Entrepreneur
MAGAZINE'S

MARKETING

**made
easy**

Additional Titles in Entrepreneur's Made Easy Series

- *Accounting and Finance for Small Business Made Easy: Secrets You Wish Your CPA Had Told You* by Robert Low
- *Business Plans Made Easy: It's Not as Hard as You Think* by Mark Henricks
- *Meetings Made Easy: The Ultimate Fix-It Guide* by Frances Micale
- *Strategic Planning Made Easy* by Fred L. Fry, Charles R. Stoner, and Laurence G. Weinzimmer
- *Advertising Without an Agency Made Easy* by Kathy J. Kobliski
- *Managing a Small Business Made Easy* by Martin E. Davis
- *Mastering Business Growth and Change Made Easy* by Jeffrey A. Hansen
- *Project Management Made Easy* by Sid Kemp

MARKETING
made easy

Kevin A. Epstein

EP Entrepreneur Press

Editorial Director: Jere Calmes
Cover Design: Beth Hansen-Winter
Editorial and Production Services: CWL Publishing Enterprises, Inc., Madison, Wisconsin, www.cwlpub.com

This publication is designed to provide accurate and authoritative information in regard to the subject matter covered. It is sold with the understanding that the publisher is not engaged in rendering legal, accounting, or other professional services. If legal advice or other expert assistance is required, the services of a competent professional person should be sought.

—From a Declaration of Principles jointly adopted by a Committee of the American Bar Association and a Committee of Publishers and Associations

ISBN 1-59918-017-0

Library of Congress Cataloging-in-Publication Data

Epstein, Kevin.
  Marketing made easy / by Kevin Epstein.
    p. cm.
  ISBN 1-59918-017-0 (9781599180175 : alk. paper)
  1. Marketing. I. Title.
    HF5415.E678 2006
    658.8--dc22

2006001861

Printed in Canada

10 09 08 07   10 9 8 7 6 5 4 3 2

Contents

Preface

Market or Die
The Money/Time/Growth Paradox

"Think like a Guerrilla, not like a Gorilla."
—VMware Marketing Programs Slogan

BEING AN ENTREPRENEUR MEANS YOU NEVER HAVE ENOUGH TIME OR money. The way to *have* enough time and money is to grow your business. But to grow your business, you need money and time—which you don't have.

This money/time/growth interdependency is the marketing paradox all entrepreneurs face. Too many entrepreneurs run themselves to death on that treadmill, like an amphetamine-driven hamster in a wheel.

The truth is that growing your business isn't about how much time and money you have; it's about how wisely you spend it. Marketing is an *amplifier* of time and money. Used correctly, marketing can make a small, smart expenditure generate large sales for your business. Used poorly, marketing can drain your time and money faster than any other business activity.

What is "poor marketing"? When a startup Internet infrastructure software company no one had heard of paid the equivalent of several staffs' yearly salary to run television commercials featuring abstract art in motion set to music and statements about life, the executive staff called it "marketing." Did the commercials generate *any* sales? No one knows. That's poor marketing.

News flash: Flashy art isn't good marketing. Abstract statements aren't good marketing. Television commercials for tiny industrial suppliers aren't good marketing. The perpetuators of those activities are spending like the gorillas of the marketplace, without understanding the common sense, guerilla resourcefulness, inventiveness, and cunning employed by talented entrepreneurial marketers. It's good guerilla thinking that *makes* companies into gorillas.

Common sense is integral to good marketing. Why? Marketing is fundamentally a process of education and awareness, teaching and sharing knowledge. Teaching and sharing are concepts most people perfected in kindergarten. Good marketing doesn't trick a would-be buyer into purchasing the wrong product; on the contrary, *good marketing ensures that the right people are led to and shown how the right products solve their needs.*

This book is about common sense, education, and awareness, seasoned with a few hints and tips picked up during two decades of executing basic marketing and lead-generation programs.

The chapters of this book are organized into three areas:

▶ **Planning:** Chapters 1 and 2 will show you how to think about your marketplace—how to assess your environment today, how to understand what you'll face in the future, and how to write a plan to market into that environment.

▶ **Doing:** Chapters 3 through 7 will show you how to turn your marketing plans into actions—how to generate awareness of your business, obtain prospective customer information, use that information to separate good from bad prospects, and focus your sales efforts on the people most likely to buy from you.

▶ **Reviewing:** Chapters 8 and 9 will show you how to continue your sales even after that initial sale—how to defend against competition, maintain customer relationships, and avoid common mistakes to keep your business growing and on track.

All chapters assume that your prospective customers are like prospective buyers the world over—like you, yourself—in that they follow a well-understood purchase process, and that marketing exists to help them through that process. If you believe marketing is about fooling or misleading people, tricking them into buying things, stop reading here and go return this book—or risk learning something in the next pages.

This book will show you the *right* way to use marketing. Each chapter can be read independently if you need a quick reference guide to a stage in the marketing process. Or you can read the book straight through from beginning to end and it will guide you through theory, strategy, planning, and execution of programs one page at a time. Either way, the book will provide you with a real-world-based, straightforward, cost-effective, step-by-step guide to creating customer awareness and sales for your business.

Whether you're a new entrepreneur seeking to establish or expand your market presence or an experienced businessperson who wants to add marketing skills to your portfolio—if you've ever wanted to be noticed, but thought you didn't have the resources to compete with the "big boys," you've found the guide you were seeking.

So read on, and understand how you can move from back room to boardroom; from garage band to global brand, using just your brain and tools you already have lying around your business. Thanks for taking the time to think before taking action—and best wishes on your campaigns.

Acknowledgments

Thanks are due to more people than can be named here, but some deserve special notice. In no particular order:

- ▶ Amy Jervis, Tasha Joan Jervis Epstein, and Elliott Alexander Jervis Epstein, who put up with quite a lot while I was writing this book and then proofread it.

- ▶ My favorite New York literary duo: Suzanne Nichols, whose amazing patience and candor guided me through literary thickets, and Jennifer Ellen Jerome, my "muse" and a far better writer than I, whose reassurance in the face of my inelegant prose was invaluable.

- ▶ Matt Wagner, agent extraordinaire, Michael Perkins, and Jamis McNiven, who introduced me to Matt and suffered though my foolish questions about publishing (and whose books are far more entertaining reading than mine).

▶ Jere Calmes, Karen Thomas, Leanne Harvey, Stephanie Harris, and the other nice folks at Entrepreneur Press for taking a risk on this project, and John Woods and colleagues at CWL Publishing Enterprises who turned the manuscript into the book you now hold.

▶ Teams past and present, who encouraged me to write this all down (and taught me quite a lot along the way).

▶ Business colleagues, friends, and reviewers: Kelly Hagen, Andrey Abramov, Pulin Sanghvi, Stephanie Spanier, Pete Sonsini, Tasha Seitz, Peter and Sandy Herz, Kevin Richardson, Eric Mulkowski, Larry Mohr, Vince Vannelli, Felda Hardymon, Philip Rosedale, Donna Novitsky, Diane Green, Jason Olim, and Kirk Bowman, who suffered through early drafts and volunteered kind words.

▶ Sara-Jane Kornblith, without whom none of this would have happened.

About the Author

Kevin Epstein is a Silicon Valley marketing executive with a Stanford MBA, a degree in high-energy nuclear physics, several technology patents in his name, founding experience at three successful small-business retail ventures, and more than 15 subsequent years of experience in guerrilla marketing tactics at such software industry high-flyers as Netscape, RealNetworks, Inktomi, and VMware.

Since 1992, his marketing programs have generated more than 5 million sales leads for companies of all sizes in all major global markets. He has spoken at seminars addressing top executives from the *Fortune* 500, has been a popular guest lecturer at the Stanford Graduate School of Business and School of Engineering, has received various awards for his impact on sales, and currently leads direct marketing efforts at the world's fastest growing large-enterprise software company.

Committed to innovation and appropriate marketing, Kevin continues to serve as an outside advisor to various venture-backed and individual entrepreneurial start-up companies. Notable prior ventures in which he has participated include CDnow (now an Amazon.com brand), Devicescape (funded by Kleiner Perkins, venture backers of Netscape), and ©Right.

Outside of the office, Kevin remains actively involved in Stanford and Brown University alumni associations, as well as local community efforts. He is also an avid sailor, swimmer, and chef. Originally from the New England area, Kevin currently resides in Northern California with his wife and two children. He may be reached at www.stupidmarketing.com.

Part One

Planning

Chapter 1

Assess Your Situation
Ready, Aim ...

"Cheshire Puss, would you tell me, please, which way I ought to go
from here?"
"That depends a good deal on where you want to get to," said the Cat.

—Lewis Carroll, *Alice in Wonderland*

I F YOU DON'T KNOW WHERE YOU ARE, IT'S MUCH HARDER TO GET TO WHERE
you want to go.

Too often, entrepreneurs launch sales and marketing efforts thinking only about where they want to go, not where they're starting from,
with unfortunate results. As the old joke says, throwing open your door
to new opportunity is a great idea unless you're on a spaceship at the time.

Good marketing begins with an understanding of the six questions: *who*
your prospective customers are, *what* these prospects want to buy, *why* you
are uniquely qualified to meet their needs, *when* and *where* you'll be ready to
do that, and *how* you can make those prospects aware of your offering.

This chapter will show you how to gain that understanding—how to
perform an assessment of the environment into which you'll launch your
marketing programs—by doing three straightforward analytical exercises.
When you've completed these analyses, you will have sufficient information
about your environment to begin to build a plan.

3

This chapter will show you how to:

- **Know your 3 Cs and 4 Ps.** Understand your current situation—your *Customers*, *Company*, and *Competitors*—and how they should influence your choice of *Product*, *Price*, *Promotion*, and *Placement*.

- **Do a SWOT analysis.** Assess your likely future environment—your *Strengths*, *Weaknesses*, *Opportunities*, and *Threats*—so that you understand how your environment may change in the future, and how to plan for that change accordingly.

- **Understand your customers' purchase process.** Ascertain your customers' likely behavior as you move (and move them) from the current to future state. *Know* which prepurchase phase your prospective customers are in, and how to prepare for and change their purchase behavior, by using your programs.

A little analysis can ensure you have the right tools and expectations, and make the difference between a great flight and a hard landing.

So before you throw open the door and launch yourself into that new market, do your homework. Be sure you know what you're about to face. A little analysis can ensure you have the right tools and expectations, and make the difference between a great flight and a hard landing.

Know Your 3 Cs and 4 Ps

The first planning step you'll need to take is to understand your *current situation*. Do the analysis to figure out whether you're in the sky or on the ground *before* you open that door and step out!

The 3 C and 4 P analysis is one of the most common analytical tools used by marketers over the last decade.

The 3 Cs stand for *Customers*, *Company*, and *Competitors*—the three semi-fixed environmental factors in your market. The 4 Ps stand for *Product*, *Price*, *Promotion*, and *Placement* (also known as *Distribution*)—the four marketing mix variables under your control.

Understanding your 3 Cs and 4 Ps should provide you with a snapshot of your marketplace—a quick overview of the "who, what, when, where, why, and how" of your customers, competitors, market, and your place in it.

Why do a 3 C and 4 P analysis? Because 90 percent of the time, you'll realize that the world isn't quite what you thought it was. Do you think you're in a comfortable position? Number one in your marketplace? Better take a look at the other companies your customers are talking to—and why. Thinking of expanding, or even launching your first offering? Better be sure you're ready to sell that type of offering, and are truly in touch with the customers who want to buy it. Shakespeare said, "Comparison is odious"—but in business, comparison is essential to survive. The worst thing you could do is spend a lot of time and effort on your marketing programs just to realize you're *not* the best positioned business to take advantage of the purchaser interest you just created.

So how do you understand and benefit from a 3 C and 4 P analysis? Take three steps: *assess*, *test*, and *adjust*.

Assess Each of the 3 Cs and 4 Ps

Start your assessment in reverse order, by defining the 4 Ps for your situation. Your 4 Ps will allow you to understand the relative position of the 3 Cs in your world. Create a new spreadsheet or table, and across the top, label the columns as follows:

▶ **Product:** The columns assessing product should discuss the attributes that customers use to compare various products—and those that you believe they would use if offered. For example, for cars, the product columns might include gas mileage, seating capacity, engine size and power, cargo space, audio options, and color options.

▶ **Price:** These columns should list average price for that type of product, as well as pricing options—One-time payment? Monthly? Loans available?

▶ **Promotion:** These columns would be a set of checkboxes, covering various promotions methods—Are coupons or rebates offered? Is the product advertised by mail, radio, seminar, webinar?

▶ **Placement:** These columns list the distribution mechanisms—Is the product in a showroom? Available for purchase by phone or Internet? Sold door-to-door?

Now add one more set of columns for the major attributes of the "first C":

▶ **Company:** These columns should address the differentiating aspects of any company in your industry. Using the auto dealer example, columns might include number of locations, quality of salespeople, quality of showrooms, consumer reputation (BBB record), yearly sales per size of company, and growth in company in recent years (measured by dollars, units, employees, or other relevant metric).

Finally, add a last set of columns for the major attributes of the "second C":

▶ **Customers:** These columns should address the differentiating aspects of customers in your industry. Using the auto example, columns might include number of prospects in the showroom on average, average age and income level of customers, price sensitivity, and other behavioral or demographic information (most of which can be obtained by watching a showroom for a day and surveying customers).

Lastly, list the competitors (and your company) in each of the rows. In each cell of the table, record their information. Then group the rows by type of customer served.

Figure 1-1 shows an example of such a chart.

Congratulations! You should now be able to see:

▶ whether your company is a lone wolf or trying to serve the same customers as everyone else.

▶ how you're performing relative to other companies in the market.

▶ whether you might want to change certain aspects of your business to perform differently.

For example, if everyone else is offering multiple colors and you're not, and their businesses are all growing and yours isn't, maybe you should reassess whether you're serving the right customers with the right offering.

Test the Relationship Between the Variables

Having built a table of the 3 Cs and 4 Ps, you can begin to make some comparisons.

Comparisons can be along one or many dimensions. For example, along a single dimension, you can simply chart yearly sales. This will show you your company's size relative to your competitors, giving you a sense of how much power they may have to spend or negotiate contracts.

Along two dimensions, you can chart sales and growth. This might alter your view of your environment—for example, showing that although you're a successful business, growth has slowed down and you're in danger of being caught by a competitor who's growing faster. If this is the case, go study that competitor. What are they doing that you aren't?

Along multiple dimensions, you can use most spreadsheets' built-in analysis tools to do "regression analysis." This involves assigning a number to each cell (for example, instead of rating companies as "good service" or "bad service," use a number between 1 and 5), then letting the analysis tool tell you which factors seem to most influence total sales. For example, a regression analysis might say that for every point of "customer service"

Product					
Company	Colored Shirts?	Disney Designs?	University Designs?	Different Weights?	Different Styles?	Interstate Delivery
Small Product Co	✗	✗		✗	✗	✗
Mr. T-Shirt				✗		
T-Shirts R Us	✗			✗		
Big T & Sons				✗		
T's & Things				✗		
Harvard Bookstore	✗	✗	Some		✗	✗
Macy's	✗	✗				✗
Nordstrom's (Teen Store)	✗	✗			✗	✗
Price					
	Avg Per Shirt	Avg # Per Deal	Volume Discounts?	Takes Credit Card	
Small Product Co	$10	3	✗	✗	
Mr. T-Shirt	$9	1		✗	
T-Shirts R Us	$14	1		✗	
Big T & Sons	$12	2		✗	
T's & Things	$5	10	✗		
Harvard Bookstore	$17	1	✗	✗	
Macy's	$25	1		✗	
Nordstrom's (Teen Store)	$35	1		✗	
Promotion					
	Coupons	News Ads	Yellow Pages	Posters	Web Site	
Small Product Co			✗		✗	
Mr. T-Shirt			✗	✗	✗	
T-Shirts R Us			✗		✗	
Big T & Sons		✗	✗	✗	✗	
T's & Things			✗			
Harvard Bookstore					✗	
Macy's	✗				✗	
Nordstrom's (Teen Store)	✗				✗	

Figure 1-1. A market assessment spreadsheet (continued on next page)

Placement				
Company	**Web Site**	**Storefront**	**College Bookstore**	**Macy's**
Small Product Co		✗		
Mr. T-Shirt	✗	✗		
T-Shirts R Us		✗		
Big T & Sons	✗	✗		
T's & Things				
Harvard Bookstore	✗	✗	✗	
Macy's	✗	✗		✗
Nordstrom's (Teen Store)	✗	✗		

Company							
	Annual Sales	**# Emp's**	**Annual Growth**	**# Shops**	**Partners**	**Repu-tation**	**Years in Shirt Biz**
Small Product Co	$1mm	3	10%	1		5-star	10
Mr. T-Shirt	$500K	2	20%	1	1	2-star	8
T-Shirts R Us	$1mm	1	20%	1		4-star	4
Big T & Sons	$250K	4	20%	1		3-star	8
T's & Things	$500k	5	20%	1		2-star	6
Harvard Bookstore	$7mm	100	3%	3	3	4-star	20
Macy's	$35mm	1000's	5%	100's	4	3-star	3
Nordstrom's (Teen Store)	$27mm	1000's	5%	100's	5	2-star	8

Customers			
	Avg # Shirts/ Deal	**Frequency of Buys**	**Other Places Shopped**	**Type Shirt**
Small Product Co	3	3	T's & Things	
Mr. T-Shirt	2	2	T's & Things	
T-Shirts R Us	1	1	T's & Things	
Big T & Sons	$250K	3	T-Shirts R Us	
T's & Things	$500k	4	T-Shirts R Us	
Harvard Bookstore	$7mm	5	T-Shirts R Us	
Macy's	$35mm	3	T-Shirts R Us	
Nordstrom's (Teen Store)	$27mm	9	T's & Things	

Figure 1-1. A market assessment spreadsheet (continued)

improvement, your overall sales will rise by 10 percent.

Lastly, test the results of your analysis by trying some experiments. If your analysis suggests that a lower price will generate a sufficient number of additional deals so that you'll make more sales, offer every tenth customer a lower price, or announce a 1-week lower price, and see what happens during your test period.

Adjust Your Business Accordingly

If your tests confirm your analysis of your world, adjust your business to perform better. Change your 4 Ps, or even the type of customer (C) that you're pursuing. You may not need significant changes—or you may realize that you have been operating a nonoptimal business for your position in the market, trying to be Nordstrom's when you're a dollar store, or vice versa.

If your tests confirm your analysis of your world, adjust your business to perform better. Change your 4 Ps, or even the type of customer (C) that you're pursuing.

Just be sure to do the 3 C and 4 P analysis *before* you create and implement your marketing programs plan, as the only thing worse than not having prospective customers aware of you is to have lots of prospective customers come and have a negative experience. It is better to be an unknown than to be a bad known or someone to avoid.

Summary: Understand your current situation via a 3 C and 4 P analysis, by obtaining data, organizing it, drawing conclusions, testing your conclusions, and adjusting your business accordingly.

- ▶ **Assess**: Collect data on the Cs and Ps for each of your competitors.
- ▶ **Test**: Use charts, regression analysis, and field tests to find meaningful differences between your and your competitors' behavior, and understand how those differences influence your respective sales.
- ▶ **Adjust**: Change your business marketing mix to best serve your true customer segment *before* you set up marketing programs to drive additional prospects.

Do a SWOT Analysis

The second planning step you'll need to take is to understand your *future environment*. Just because you're in that orbiting spaceship now doesn't mean you always will be—and letting a competitor beat you to that door because they were ready for landing could cost you the sale.

The first letters of the acronym SWOT stand for *Strengths* and *Weaknesses*—factors internal to the company. The last letters of the acronym stand for *Opportunities* and *Threats*—factors external to the company. Whereas the prior 3 C and 4 P analysis is a market snapshot in time, a SWOT analysis is a measure of your company's innate capabilities, and the forces surrounding your company. A SWOT analysis can help you to understand how your environment is likely to change, and how well prepared your business is to handle those changes.

For example, is your business a great producer of low-cost goods? That's a great strength, but an upcoming threat might be low-cost offshore manufacturing becoming available to your competitors. Do you have a weakness in that your business depends on a consulting company to install your products? A corresponding opportunity might be to develop a consulting reseller business. The SWOT analysis doesn't map your position; it only maps a balance of the capabilities you have against the challenges you face.

So how do you understand *your* SWOT profile? Consider each of the pairs in turn.

Strengths	**Weaknesses**
Opportunities	**Threats**

Figure 1-2. SWOT analysis map

Strengths and Weaknesses

Strengths and weaknesses refer to the internal capabilities of your company. Like any machine, you need to consider whether the parts of your company will stand up to the work you are tasking it with. So ask: For your market, what are the critical success factors? How does your business rate on each aspect—is it a strength or a weakness?

Common factors include:

Like any machine, you need to consider whether the parts of your company will stand up to the work you are tasking it with.

▶ **Operations:** your ability to deliver your product or service. Are you faster? Higher quality? More local? Friendlier?

▶ **Customer service and support:** post-sale support. Are you reachable? Speak their language? Return phone calls?

▶ **Sales:** ability to sell. Can you make a compelling case? Can you present?

- ▶ **Channel:** strength of distribution channel. How many places or ways can people buy your product or service? What forms of payment do you accept?
- ▶ **Finances:** financial condition of your business, ability to weather bad times, offer credit to customers
- ▶ **Research and development:** ability of your business to create new offerings
- ▶ **Marketing:** ability of your business to efficiently alert and guide the right set of prospects
- ▶ **Executive vision:** ability of your business to accurately predict changes

Opportunities and Threats

Opportunities and threats refer to the external market conditions your business will face. What market changes can you see happening that would be challenging to your business? What changes could help your business (and possibly hinder others)?

Common market factors include:

- ▶ **Regulatory issues:** changes in government rules. As a lawn care service, do you care that your town is about to ban leaf-blowers?
- ▶ **Consumer issues:** general economic slowdown or acceleration, or that in your area. Will people losing jobs when a big company shuts down mean fewer paying for your lawn care service?
- ▶ **New technologies:** changes in the behavior of consumers as they change solutions. Will more people be buying their own lawnmowers, as lawnmowers become easier to use?
- ▶ **Customer loyalty:** degree of customer retention
- ▶ **Sales volatility:** amount of sales dependent on a single deal or calendar period. Do all your sales happen in the spring?

The Analysis

Once you've written down your strengths, weaknesses, opportunities, and threats, you will be one step closer to a marketing programs plan. Have a weakness? Use marketing to shift customer focus on to areas where you're stronger. Is there an upcoming threat? Use your marketing programs (and associated product and company strengths) to take advantage of new opportunities. If you're more expensive than any other competitor, market your higher-quality offerings, or exploit other strengths. If you're a lawn care professional and people are buying lawnmowers, go into mower use training and repair.

In the end, the environmental situation will be what it will be—but your position in the market will depend on what you make of the situation. Will you surf the tidal wave or brace yourself and try not to be sucked under? As the old adage goes, if life hands you lemons, make lemonade. The offensive or defensive choice is yours—but making a conscious choice and plan is the starting point for success.

Summary: A SWOT analysis lets you prepare for your future, by assessing your business's strengths relative to the critical skills needed to succeed in the industry, and your market position relative to the market's movement. Use the results of SWOT to act to make best use of your strengths and position.

- ▶ **Strengths and weaknesses:** Assess your internal capabilities relative to the skills needed to succeed in the market you've chosen.
- ▶ **Opportunities and threats:** Assess the market conditions.
- ▶ **The best defense is a good offense.** Always be attempting to build the strengths needed to seize the next market opportunity, and your weaknesses may not matter.

Understand Your Customer Purchase Process

The third and last planning step you'll need to take before beginning to *implement* your marketing programs is to understand your prospective customers' likely behavior when *confronted* with your marketing programs. This will allow you to plan your timelines and efforts accordingly—after all, there's no sense in rushing out that door if your customers aren't going to be ready to meet you.

The customer purchase process refers to the several distinct phases *every* buyer of a product or service passes through in his or her prepurchase thinking.

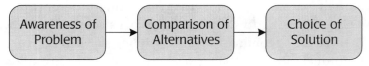

Figure 1-3. Customer purchase process

Marketing is designed to facilitate, influence, or accelerate the potential buyer's progress through those phases.

Consider:

- ▶ How does marketing for breakfast cereal, where the purchase process takes less than five minutes, differ from that for automobiles, where the process can take weeks to months?

- ▶ If you're marketing automobiles, knowing how people purchase, could you adjust some of the Ps (for example, price) to accelerate purchase?

- ▶ Alternatively, if you wanted to delay the purchase process so that you could come out with a better product than a competitor, could you adjust any Ps (for example, promotion) to convince customers to wait?

Ask yourself: What's involved in each of the customer phases, and how would your marketing programs apply to each?

Awareness

If you don't think you're sick, it's a lot harder for anyone to sell you a cure. The first phase of the purchase process involves helping your potential purchaser to recognize that there's a problem they need to fix. Sometimes, problem recognition is generated by social dynamics, or by the prospective purchasers themselves. For example, a customer for deodorant may recognize that they need that product because they themselves realize or are told by friends that they smell bad. Other times, problem recognition is generated by your marketing program. For example, commercial TV or print advertising implies that deodorant creates greater sex appeal, popularity, success, and well-being.

Of course, if you're the first person to create problem recognition in the potential purchaser's mind, you have an advantage: you can set the agenda. You can tailor the scope of the perceived problem to fit your offering. For example, NyQuil cold medicine makes you drowsy... so NyQuil's marketing targets people who want a better night's sleep, and doesn't acknowledge or spend time on the challenge of people who wish to make their sneezing go away while still remaining alert.

If you're the first person to create problem recognition in the potential purchaser's mind, you have an advantage: you can set the agenda.

Put simply: people who learn about problems from you will seek solutions from you as well. So understand where your prospective customers are in their problem recognition. Do they know they need your product? If so, spend less on programs in this area, and more on programs to influence comparison and choice phases. *Know where your customers are, and you'll know what you need to do to move them to purchase.*

Comparison

If no one knows your company exists, they can't buy anything from you. The second phase of the purchase process involves the potential purchaser acquiring alternative solutions to their problem, comparing the solutions on a set of criteria, and narrowing down the set of possible solutions to a specific set of purchase alternatives.

For example, prospective deodorant customers must understand available deodorant options (roll-on, spray) and then compare what's important to them (price, scent), then choose among brands.

Marketing managers compete for awareness for two reasons: basic inclusion in the purchase consideration set and for the agenda-setting reasons previously mentioned.

To gain awareness, you have to reach the customers with your message—via billboard, mail, phone, or other communication. If you can get close enough to a customer to capture their information (email, phone number) and then reach them repeatedly, directly, and personally with your message, benefits, and competitive information, you can remain in their consideration and choice set to become a viable purchase alternative for them. Then you can try to sell them something.

Put simply: people who know about you, and why you're useful to them, will buy things from you.

Put simply: people who know about you, and why you're useful to them, will buy things from you. The closer to them you are, the more you can communicate. So be sure you understand where they are in their comparison process. If they're just starting, you can set the agenda, like Nyquil, dictating to them how they *should* be comparing products. If you're late to the comparison, just be sure you meet their criteria—explain how your product fits their needs.

Choice of Solution

If prospective customers know about you and believe you meet their needs better than anyone else, they'll buy from you. The challenge is focusing your sales efforts on the right customers.

Who are the right customers? The right customers are people whom your marketing programs have prequalified and educated about your product's unique benefits. These are people who aren't even thinking about making a *choice* of solution, because you've educated them such that in their minds, you're the only reasonable option to buy.

Why are these educated customers the right customers? These people are the right customers because they won't waste your time. When you sell to them, all of your time will be explaining the benefits of *your* product, not doing general education on the solution (education that equally benefits your competition). You'll be explaining why to buy *your* product, not why to buy. You won't be attempting to force sales onto people where, for reasons of price, quality, or applicability, they don't believe you're the best to meet their needs.

So concentrate your marketing efforts on the right customers. If you're a high-price, high-quality company, don't market to the target audience of dollar stores, and vice versa. Like trying to teach a pig to dance, it wastes your time (and theirs), and annoys the pig.

Summary: The customer purchase process defines prospective customers' path from "zero knowledge of you" to "purchase of your offering." Knowing where your customers are in that process will help you drive them to where you want them to be—caring about your offering, buying from *you*.

- ▶ **Problem recognition:** alerting the prospective customer to a problem they need fixed
- ▶ **Information search:** providing the prospective customer with your business offering as a solution to their problem
- ▶ **Evaluation of alternatives:** explaining to now-educated prospective customers why your solution is the uniquely best qualified for their situation

Parting Thought: Avoiding "Ready, Fire, Aim"

The single greatest cause of marketing program failure isn't lack of funding, lack of time, or even poor execution. The single greatest cause of program failure is lack of planning—and it's a common failure.

Why is lack of planning such a common point of failure? Because great entrepreneurs have a bias toward action. You know that you'd rather get something done today, instead of putting it off until tomorrow. You believe in your business, that's why you're an entrepreneur. So why shouldn't you use your best judgment and launch those marketing programs? Why spend the extra time doing analysis?

The answer is that speed can kill. As previously noted, bad marketing can be worse than no marketing—it can actively take the investment from your company and tell prospective customers why they *shouldn't* buy from you. Organized thinking forces you to pause, and reconsider all of the variables before launching.

So take the time to be a marketing ACE—to *Assess*, *Check* your plan, and *then Execute* it. You'll be more assured of having all the parts work together, without missing any details, and being on the road to success. You don't need to spend months or years on this analysis—it can be done in a few weeks, or sometimes days at a general level. But take 10 percent of your marketing programs' time to plan—you won't regret it.

Chapter 2

Plan
Before You Jump, Ask "How High"

"Act in haste … repent at leisure."

—Proverb

IF YOU CAN PLAN BUT CAN'T EXECUTE ON YOUR PLANS, YOU'RE A DREAMER, not an entrepreneur.

Even brilliant would-be entrepreneurs, who understand their prospective customers' needs *and* have a great strategy, can fail at marketing. It's critical to strike a balance between planning and execution. *Understanding* isn't *doing*.

Success depends on translating your strategic vision into a series of tactical actions. When pitting "saying" skills against "doing" skills in building a business, the people who can "do" will always win.

This chapter will give you the tools you need to start down the path of "doing." You'll learn how to answer the three hard questions every entrepreneurial marketer faces when trying to translate their strategic vision into real marketing programs. Then you'll get a template for combining those answers and your strategic analysis from Chapter 1 into an actionable plan. By the end of the chapter, you'll know how to:

▶ **Balance quantity versus quality of leads.** Understand whether you need to reach wide or deep with your marketing programs

- **Choose goals.** Know exactly how much marketing you need to do to generate the amount of sales you seek
- **Track and measure programs.** Know if your marketing programs are working, and where they could improve
- **Build your marketing plan.** Put it all together in a form that's right for *you*

Remember, it's not enough to have an offering that "anyone" could buy: To succeed as an entrepreneur, you have to sell your offering to someone.

Remember, it's not enough to have an offering that "anyone" could buy: To succeed as an entrepreneur, you have to sell your offering to *someone.* So don't procrastinate. Make the difficult choices about which opportunities you'll pursue, in what order, and adjust your marketing plans accordingly *before* spending time and money. You'll end up with much better results.

Balancing Quantity versus Quality of Leads

The first planning decision you'll need to make is that of quantity versus quality of leads.

Should your time and money be spent in a concentrated fashion, courting a few potentially extremely valuable customers? Or should you cast a wide net, spreading your contact information as far as possible, in the hopes of catching a larger number of less individually valuable customers?

The answers depend on the stage your business is in, the breadth and sophistication of your audience, your price-point, and the complexity of what you're selling. For example, consider the marketing of expensive, complex items such as passenger jets, or nuclear power plant turbines. The *volume* of prospective customer contacts generated by your marketing is less important than reaching the correct *high-quality* contacts, with a very deep and sophisticated marketing approach. For jets or turbines, relatively few people are critical to the purchasing decision. It's more important to reach them than thousands of people who don't matter.

Conversely, for inexpensive, simple items such as software-based MP3 players, volume of buyers is important. Marketing for maximum market *share* and end-consumer awareness creates success.

To understand the tradeoffs, consider:

- Quality (higher cost per lead)
- Quantity (lower cost per lead)
- Why the tradeoff exists and matters

18

Understand those three aspects, and you'll understand when each marketing approach should take precedence, and what "taking precedence" actually entails in tactical terms.

Quality (Higher Cost per Lead)

When product price is higher, complexity of product or installation is higher, or value per deal is concentrated in a few larger deals, the quality of leads has a direct correlation to sales efficiency and success. The valuable audience you need to market to will consist of only a few specific individuals. In this situation, accurate targeting of marketing efforts is of more importance than the volume of contacts created. Why? Cost. It's likely that the purchase process will be extensive and extended—that each prospective customer will require customized, in-depth education about your offering and its benefit to them.

So it's important to expend marketing efforts on only the correct contacts. More research and planning time spent before programs launch, and investment in higher-value marketing programs focused on a select few individuals will result in more revenue.

Consider these examples of how such tightly targeted marketing programs might differ in implementation from more mass-market-oriented programs:

- ▶ **E-mail:** Instead of using mass-mail-merge and large purchased generic lists, send a personal e-mail to the target contact from an analyst related to the target company, with a "cc" to the marketing or salesperson from your company being introduced.

- ▶ **Seminars:** Don't hold large, anonymous hotel or stadium-based events; rather, arrange in-person meetings or small executive-level forums or individual lunches.

- ▶ **Direct mail:** Instead of generic postcards, send direct mail via FedEx, with a personal note from you, as your company's CEO, on wedding-invitation-quality cards.

- ▶ **Materials:** Instead of generic case studies, use specific examples as applied to the target company's own systems, cost structure, and environment, showing detailed knowledge and understanding of the most important issues, and how your solution helps.

In sum, high-touch personal marketing will always improve the quality of your leads if initially directed at the appropriate market. But such marketing is expensive on a cost-per-lead basis. You won't be exposed to as many people, so success depends significantly on the ability to tightly define the target audience prior to spending on them.

Quantity (Lower Cost per Lead)

When the product price is relatively low, number of units sold is relatively high, and individual deal size is relatively small, large numbers of sales must be made for the business to show revenue growth. In these circumstances, your marketing goal should be a *lower cost per lead*, so that you maximize the number of people you reach on your fixed budget. Usually a quantity-driven product has a short purchase process, and one where decision authority is minimally permuted within an organization: *only one person needs to be convinced of your product's value for you to make a sale.*

Marketing efforts can thus be relatively straightforward and minimally customized, using larger volume and lower cost-per-target programs. Standard marketing programs might include:

▶ E-mail to lists purchased from magazines or trade shows

▶ Webinars or open seminars by city

▶ Direct-mail postcards

▶ Mass-produced materials, with generic case studies by industry

A specific message applies perfectly to a narrow set of individuals; a general message applies less perfectly to everyone.

With the above caveat in mind, allowing your marketing message to depersonalize—to regress to the mean—can actually have a beneficial effect on lead flow, as your programs seek to attract as many as possible of the specified (large) segments. Put differently, a specific message applies perfectly to a narrow set of individuals; a general message applies less perfectly to everyone. So when choosing between quantity and quality, err on the side of *quantity* (within limits)—as by giving yourself more options when selecting prospective customers, you will likely increase your overall revenue.

Why It Matters

More is not always better. Lead generation costs money, and if you generate too many leads—in that your ability to follow-up on leads is overwhelmed—valuable leads are ignored and lost as opportunities.

Since the only thing worse than a prospective customer who *hasn't* heard about you is one who *wanted* to buy from you and was ignored (as far as they could tell, you couldn't be bothered to contact them and take their money), you need to balance the value of annoyed lost customers against nonacquired customers.

Summary: How do you choose between quantity and quality? Assess the number of prospective customers, as determined by product price, total volume of likely sales, and individual purchase size.

▶ *Quality:* when there are few customers for a high-priced, low-volume, large-deal offering

▶ *Quantity:* when there are many customers for a low-priced, high-volume, small-deal offering

▶ *Err on the side of quantity.* It's easier to dig through muck to find jewels than to not have the jewels in the first place.

Choosing Goals

The second planning decision you'll need to make is that of how many leads you'll need.

Do you know how many contacts you'll need your marketing programs to produce for you to reach your sales target? The answer is related to *close* and *conversion* rates—the percentage of original prospects that become paying customers—which are in turn directly related to marketing effectiveness. After all, the perfect "sales funnel" would be shaped like a pipe—100 percent of people who learned about your offering would quickly move straight through to purchase.

Unfortunately, most sales funnels are more V-shaped: prospective customers are lost to inefficient marketing, dropping out of the funnel as they progress through the marketing and sales steps. (See Figure 2-1.)

But as long as these loss rates are known, desired lead quantities can be calculated.

The funnel math you'd use to calculate lead quantities, associated programs spending, and consequent marketing budget is obtained by working backwards from the desired end result, to understand your sales deals need, leads need, contacts need, and thus marketing reach and programs need.

This philosophy can be outlined as follows.

1. Understand how big a sales challenge you're facing.

▶ Imagine a situation where you want your marketing programs to help you sell $1 million worth of product in one quarter (3 months). (This million-dollar number is set by first determining the available market and possible penetration.)

▶ You know that the average sales deal size for your company is $25K. You can find this number by looking at prior quarters of sales data.

Most sales funnels are more V-shaped: prospective customers are lost to inefficient marketing, dropping out of the funnel as they progress through the marketing and sales steps.

21

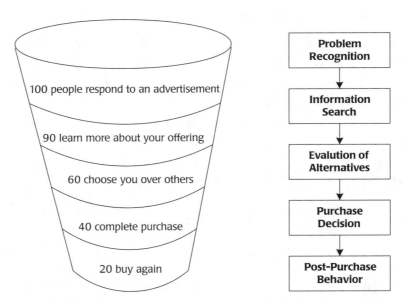

Figure 2-1. Sales funnel

Thus, your sales challenge is that you must close 40 deals per quarter ($1mm/$25K = 40), or about 10 deals every three weeks, to meet your sales target of $1 million.

2. Calculate How Many Qualified Leads You Need to Meet the Sales Challenge

▶ You know that the average sales deal size for your company is $25K. Your known conversion rate on marketing programs in your company is that 3 percent of everyone who tries your product (your definition of a qualified sales lead) becomes a purchaser. You can find conversion rates by using industry averages, or, more directly, by examining past records of the contact information provided to you at the point where a prospect did a trial and comparing it with your sales contact information. Over a one-quarter period, you should have enough data to establish a baseline conversion rate.

Thus, you now know that you need 1,333 people (40 deals/3% = 1,333) evaluating your product to produce 40 deals.

3. Calculate How Many Contacts You Need to Obtain the Requisite Number of Qualified Leads

▶ You know that 5 percent of people who click through to your web-based "landing page" evaluate a product (based on clicks on the "Try Now" tracking URL on your landing page, evaluated over the last quarter).

Thus, you now know that you need 26,666 people reaching your landing page (1,333 people/5% = 26,660) to produce 1,333 people doing evaluations.

4. Calculate How Broad a Reach Your Initial Marketing Program Must Have To Generate The Requisite Number of Contacts

▶ You know that e-mail from your company yields a 1 percent click through; advertisements yield a 0.2 percent click through, and so forth, based on prior measurement.

Thus, you need 2.7mm e-mails sent, or 13mm ads, or some combination of these and other marketing programs (based on least expensive cost per impression and availability of the number of impressions in the targeted vehicles and venues you'll be using) to generate the 26,660 contacts, 1,333 evaluations, and subsequent 40 deals.

The end result should give you a sense of how much marketing you'll need to do, and of what types. Of course, if your funnel math shows you that the cost of the programs to get the leads you think you'll need to sell $1 million is in fact significantly more than $1 million, you have a larger business problem. But at least you've made that discovery before starting to spend the money!

Summary: How do you choose your goals? Work backwards from the sales you'll need.

▶ How many deals do you need to reach the sales dollar target?

▶ How many leads do you need to produce that number of deals?

▶ How many contacts do you need to produce that number of leads?

▶ How broad a reach must you achieve with marketing to obtain that many contacts... and how much will that cost?

Tracking and Measuring Programs

The third planning decision you'll need to make is that of how you'll track and measure your programs. Before starting any program, ask yourself: How will I be able to tell which programs led prospective customers to me? How can I tell who of my prospective customers investigated my offerings further, and who turned away quickly (and why)? How will I know who ended up buying, and what they bought, and how it related to the original marketing program that brought them to me?

If the results of a marketing program can't be measured, it doesn't exist. The smaller the available budget, the more crucial the ability to measure results, to understand what worked and what didn't, and alter or justify future investment as appropriate. To be successful, understand:

- ▶ Where prospective customers come from (before they find you)
- ▶ What prospective customers do next (once they've found you)
- ▶ What they buy from you (if anything)

Implement the following tactics to gain that understanding.

Where Prospective Customers Came From

The first link in the measurement chain is the link between your marketing program action and your prospective customers' response. You forge the first link in the chain by giving every program and vehicle you use a unique identifier—ideally one that can be tracked in an automated way, without prospective customer involvement, thus increasing the reliability of your tracking results.

Common examples of unique identifiers include:

- ▶ **Unique web URLs:** When sending e-mail, or handing out CDs, or providing any material with a web link on it (even printed materials), create a unique tracking URL. This can range from complex if hidden (the e-mail says "click on www.yourco.com," when the underlying URL looks like http://www.yourco.com/offer/1558/special.jsp) to simple (the postcard says "come to www.yourco.com/specialoffer"). Any visitors to those unique URLs can be credited to your program.
- ▶ **Unique phone numbers:** As with the approach used with URLs, when printing phone numbers, consider a number unique to the offer. At a minimum, you should have a special extension ("dial 1-800-555-1212

Before starting any program, ask yourself: How will I be able to tell which programs led prospective customers to me?

24

x123"). Ideally you'd have a dedicated number that was different from your company's main line ("dial 1-800-555-1313") or even a unique number that was easily remembered ("dial 1-800-Try-MyCo").

▶ **Unique response-card codes:** Since response cards are being physically returned to your company, they should have preprinted bar codes indicating their source—which marketing program or mailing originally contained them. Even low-tech solutions are possible—for example, using different colors or graphic designs on handouts used at different events, if applying a physical code is impossible.

▶ **Unique referral codes:** If physical attachment of codes or use of unique phone numbers is absolutely impossible—for example, in verbal campaigns or walk-in campaigns, such as radio ads—then incentive-driven referral statements can be used. "Tell them you heard about them on 95.5 WBRU, and get 5 percent off your bill." Alternatively, prompted responses can be obtained—when people call in, your telemarketing rep can ask either "where did you hear about us," or "did you hear about us from any of the following sources [list]?"

There is no magic formula to unique identifiers. Create them in any form that you want, from color of coupons to radio ID tags embedded in trial products that can be exchanged for full versions. But don't neglect to forge the first link in the chain, for without it the rest of your analysis is meaningless.

What Prospective Customers Want or Do Next

The second link in the measurement chain is the link between prospective customers' initial response and subsequent action. You attracted customers to you with a message. Was the message consistent with the details they subsequently discover? Can they obtain answers to their questions, and do those answers move them toward your product as they progress through consideration and evaluation phases of the purchase process? Or are you losing people who felt they were lured in under false pretenses, or who grow frustrated attempting to extract the information they need to make a purchase from you?

You forge the second link in the chain by attaching information about subsequent customer actions and requests to their primary response action.

You forge the second link in the chain by attaching information about subsequent customer actions and requests to their primary response action. Common examples of subsequent tracking include:

▶ **Web site flow metrics:** Once the prospective customer reaches a unique "landing page" on your site, directed there by a unique URL in an e-mail or elsewhere, the tracking shouldn't stop. Do they choose the "Try Now" button/link? The "Learn More" link? What choice do they make on the next page? How long do they stay on the page between choices? When do they finally exit your site? By analyzing traffic patterns, you can detect and remove barriers to the purchase process.

▶ **Telephone menu choices:** As is the case with web site flow metrics, the same analysis can be applied to menu or voice-driven telephone recorded information or fax-back systems—often with the added benefit that with caller-ID, a unique index can be established without any need for caller input.

▶ **Prompted telemarketing or telesales rep choices:** If your response leads prospective customers to a live interaction with a telemarketing or telesales representative, the rep can be presented with a log in which to record questions, as well as a script for offering a standard set of choices (then recorded). "Thanks for calling. Can I send you a whitepaper? Would you like to try our product? Would you like pricing information?"

▶ **Point of sale credit card cross references:** If your prospective customer provides their credit card for any purpose—a minor other sale, or for lookup information (such as is used by the automated check-in kiosks at the airport), you can cross-reference to other related purchases or behaviors (how often they have checked in at this airport, for what types of destinations, and how often).

If you're able to track behavior that enables you to see where friction occurs in the purchase process, you're measuring the right things.

As is the case with unique ID tracking, the exact method used is less important than the fit of the method to your prospective customers' purchasing process. If you're able to track behavior that enables you to see where friction occurs in the purchase process, you're measuring the right things.

What Did Prospective Customers Actually Buy?

The third and final link in the measurement chain is the link between all of your lead generation activities, from initial touch through follow-up and maturation activities, to final purchase. After all of your work attracting and educating people, did they buy, and how much? What aspects of what you did were associated with higher-end buyers, and what aspects of what you did ended up having apparently no effect, rarely being associated with a sale? Did any of your programs have a *negative* effect on sales?

You forge the third link in the chain by associating specific sales with specific sets of marketing programs, doing statistical analysis on this set of data (correlation, regression testing) as described in Chapter 4. Common ways to link sales back to marketing programs include:

▶ **Direct linkage:** If you have access to a master index at point of sale—for example, if you're using e-mail address domain name as your master marketing data index, the common bit of information collected at each activity, and e-mail address domain name is also captured at sale—then you're done. You've forged the third link.

▶ **Rebates:** If you don't have access to a master index at sale—for example, your customers buy through resellers, who don't reveal end-customer data to you—then you'll need a method to convince the customers to return their master index data to you. Common methods include "product registration" (for warrantees, updates, and information), rebates (for explicit cash rewards), or contests (similar incentive)—all of which involve end users directly submitting information to you.

▶ **Surveys:** If you don't have access to a master index at sale, but also haven't been able to implement the first two links in your chain, you can always use a survey. While imprecise, it does directly touch end customers (you mail it directly to them), is uniform, and links programs to purchase. It is biased toward recency (customers better remember recent programs) and size (flashy programs are better remembered), but may still provide some useful data.

Summary: How should you measure and track? Put measurements in place in three areas.

▶ Where prospective customers come from
▶ What prospects do once they've found you
▶ What they actually buy

Build Your Marketing Programs Plan

Having made your decisions on quantity tradeoffs, calculated your desired reach, and understood your measurement options, your last step is to create a plan.

The plan is a summary of your thinking, starting with your analysis of the market today, continuing with your views of how things might change, and documenting the steps you need to take to continue to attract and sell to customers in that environment.

The plan is a summary of your thinking, starting with your analysis of the market today.

27

Your plan will have eight parts:

- ▶ Situation analysis and conclusions
- ▶ Objective
- ▶ Plan
- ▶ Key elements and dependencies
- ▶ Timeline
- ▶ Resources required
- ▶ Cash budget
- ▶ Metric and goal

Taking the time and effort to write down your plan lets you stop and think about "the big picture," ensure your actions are consistent with your goals, and verify that you're taking action in an efficient manner.

Don't worry—eight parts may seem intimidating, but your plan doesn't need to be long or complex. Many of the sections will be only a sentence or two. But the discipline is useful. Taking the time and effort to write down your plan lets you stop and think about "the big picture," ensure your actions are consistent with your goals, and verify that you're taking action in an efficient manner.

So what really goes into each section? The following descriptions and examples should get you started on *your* plan. See also Appendix A.

Situation Analysis and Conclusions

Start with a brief recap of your situation analysis and conclusions. What did your 3C/4P analysis tell you about your current market and your place in it? Summarize for each of the seven variables using the chart described in Chapter 1. What did your SWOT analysis tell you about upcoming market changes, and your readiness to face them? Use this section of your marketing plan to summarize the state of your market world and what you want to do about your situation in a few sentences.

For example, you might present your 3C/4P analysis, showing that you're the low-price, high-volume producer of buggy-whips. Yet your SWOT analysis shows that the overall market is getting smaller. Your conclusions are that you're going to need to raise prices and focus on a small group of wealthy buggy owners.

Objective

Given your conclusions in section 1, with specific reference to the customer purchase process and your lead calculations, what are your goals?

For example, you've calculated that to make your sales target of $1 million of buggy-whip sales, you need to do only 10 large deals with horse race-tracks, so your leads and impressions goals are only 3 million impressions. But the impressions must be targeted at that small set of race-track owners, and must focus on the "consideration" stage of the purchase process (they're already aware of your product, but don't consider you a supplier to race-tracks; they need to be re-educated and convinced).

Plan

Given the type of objective listed, and the necessary impressions per type of marketing touches needed, set up a series of programs to obtain those touches (see Chapter 3 for more detail). Provide an overview of how the various programs will interact to achieve your objective.

For example, "Banner ads will push webinar registration. Follow-up e-mail will offer whitepaper."

Key Elements and Dependencies

Are there critical elements of your plan? For example, you must send e-mail prior to your webinar, because the e-mail is how people will learn of the webinar. Is the webinar essential, because it is the only opportunity to demonstrate the new prototype buggy-whip?

List out your critical elements. This is the section that should serve as your critical checklist when you're under pressure later.

Timeline

When does each program need to be completed? What does that imply about when each has to launch—and in turn, what does that imply about when each needs materials written, printed, delivered, or created? Include extra "recovery" time for when your suppliers (printers, poster hangers) miss their deadlines. Work backwards from the final result, and you'll realize you're already late.

Resources Required

What will be needed to complete your programs? How many hours of your time, external agencies (such as e-mail list brokers), and others will be required?

Cash Budget

What's the line-by-line cash budget needed?

Metric and Goal

Referring to the prior section on measurement, and your objectives, what is your concrete goal in terms of number of people and type of people that you hope to reach? How will you know if you're successful?

Summary: How can you avoid failure? Measure sales, and build in measurement methods.

- ▶ Understand what to measure—and always measure the program's linkage to sales.
- ▶ Build ways of measuring different factors into your marketing program.
- ▶ Change one variable—one aspect of your program—at a time, then repeat and re-measure.

Parting Thought: Asking "How High"?

S ometimes the plan is as important as your results in determining success. If you plan and fail, you should be able to understand that failure and learn from it.

You should now have a great tactical plan to go along with your great strategy. All that you have to do now is implement that plan. But sometimes the plan is as important as your results in determining success. If you plan and fail, you should be able to understand that failure and learn from it. The failure becomes a success. Conversely, if you didn't plan and still succeed, all you've done was win the lottery. You have no way of knowing whether anything you did contributed to that success, or whether you got lucky—and you have no way of being sure that you can repeat the success.

So plan. That way, whatever happens, you'll still gain information to use as you move forward—and that's a definite win.

30

Part Two

Doing

Chapter 3

Create Awareness I: Make Them See You
Tell Your Friends (and They'll Tell Their Friends)

"There is only one thing in the world worse than being talked about, and that is not being talked about."

—Oscar Wilde

I F NO ONE KNOWS YOUR BUSINESS EXISTS, IT SOON WON'T. HISTORY SHOWS that too often entrepreneurs who have great technology lose to entrepreneurs who have great marketing. The saying "if you build a better mousetrap, the world will beat a path to your door" is a lie. The truth is that to *sell* mousetraps, you must first create *awareness* that your mousetraps *exist*.

Bad marketers attempt to create awareness by spending heavily and indiscriminately, pushing their message onto prospective consumers and innocent bystanders alike. National print advertising campaigns, billboards, radio or television commercials, and other unmeasured high-cost "brand building" activities are classic examples of tactics employed by nonentrepreneurs with money to waste.

There is a better way to create awareness. This chapter and the next will show you how to use existing social phenomena and technology to reach more prospective customers than a Superbowl ad reaches, faster, and for a fraction of the cost. The difference between the two chapters is that of proactive versus reactive awareness generation—the difference between throwing spears and setting out nets when hunting for customers.

▶ This chapter contains techniques for *proactive* awareness generation—awareness-generation tactics that involve actively seeking out potential users of the products or services you provide. If the type of people you'd want to sell to don't even realize that they have a problem or specific need—for example, if you were the first person to market a house-cleaning service in an area where people had traditionally cleaned their own houses—you should use these types of tactics. You'll be throwing spears at moving targets.

▶ The next chapter contains techniques for *reactive* awareness generation—awareness-generation tactics that involve ensuring that potential users seeking solutions can find *you*. If you are engaging in a business that is serving an already well-understood need—for example, you're providing another taxi service in a city where taxis are used—you should use *these* types of tactics. You'll be setting out nets to herd and catch already motivated potential buyers.

See Figure 3-1 to understand if you need to read this chapter first.

By the end of this chapter, you will know how to gain awareness among less-aware customers quickly and cost effectively.

	Customer may not even be aware they have an issue to be addressed	Customer is actively looking for a solution to their issue
Minimal Impact Reaches Many	**Start with Family:** Word of Mouth, Viral Programs	**Be News**
	Alert Your Community: Affinity Marketing, Blogvertising	**Help Them Find You:** Directories
	Hang Out Your Shingle: Advertising	**Throw a Party:** Live Events
Maximal Impact Reaches Fewer	**Get Personal and Direct:** Mail, Telemarketing	**Build Instant Credibility:** Partnering and Comarketing

Figure 3-1. Marketing activities

This chapter will show you how to:

▶ **Start with family:** Generate awareness via word-of-mouth and viral marketing.

▶ **Alert your community:** Generate awareness via interest groups, blogs, and created groups.

▶ **Hang out your shingle:** Generate awareness via mass advertising—signage, print, radio, TV.

▶ **Get personal and direct:** Generate awareness via direct touch, using mail and telemarketing.

These are tactics any entrepreneur can use, without a large budget or the assistance of a marketing agency—so don't delay, try these today!

Start with Family

If you ever sold anything as a child—lemonade from a stand, chocolates or magazines for school, tickets to team events, *anything*—you knew that you could always rely on your family for a sale.

As you grew up, maybe family members couldn't always support your business through direct purchases—but when you bought your first car, or first television, or first stereo system, you probably asked the advice of family or friends.

Fact: In an information-rich environment, you *and everyone you know* depend on friends and family to help filter input. Smart businesses know that this social filtering, influence, and feedback effect happens, and over the last 50 years have taken advantage of social connections and associated reputational "buzz" to sell everything from Tupperware to shampoo to magazine subscriptions.

Yet reputations aren't just random—they can be built. Whether you call it "Viral Marketing" or just word of mouth, by starting with friends and family, you can generate reputational awareness of your better mousetrap. Friends and family aren't just blood, they're cheap and effective marketing targets. Consider the following tactics.

In an information-rich environment, you and everyone you know *depend on friends and family to help filter input.*

Word of Mouth

What is it? Word of mouth describes social network effects *not* carried by an intermediate product, but actually implemented directly. If you create a marketing program that causes each customer or prospect to *directly tell other* *potential customers about your offering* (in a positive way), you're doing word-of-mouth marketing.

When should you use it? Word of mouth is effective when your product fosters conversation. Visible, design-differentiated products tend to have this effect. For example, if you can see the product (Apple's iPod, your friend's clothing or haircut), you may ask where someone bought it.

When should you not use it? Word of mouth can maintain or distort your message—it's not necessarily a good medium for complex messages.

How much should it cost per person reached? Word of mouth is a subtle vehicle, and so should have minimal cost per person reached. If you send e-mail announcing your business to ten friends, and ask them to each send to ten friends (and so on), it should cost you nothing. If you choose to add incentive ("Tell your friends, and you'll both get a discount when you bring in this e-mail"), the costs can increase, but should still be relatively cheap on a per-person basis.

Viral Marketing

If you create a marketing program that causes each customer to make at least two more potential customers aware of your offering by using or distributing your offering (or related material), you're doing viral marketing.

What is it? *Viral marketing* is a term created in the late 1990s to describe social network effects carried by an intermediate product. In other words, if you create a marketing program that causes each customer to make at least two more potential customers aware of your offering *by using or distributing your offering (or related material)*, you're doing viral marketing. For example, if you are sent something in an envelope whose quality you admire, and the envelope's rear face has a statement, "Like this envelope? Go to www.envelopes.com to learn more," you may be "infected" by the envelope company's message, passed by one of their customers to a potential customer.

When should you use it? Viral marketing is effective when your product has a built-in excuse to be delivered to other people. For example, e-mail, phone calls, envelopes, and business cards are all possible viral vectors because each is seen by potential other users of the offering.

When should you not use it? Viral marketing doesn't work if it's excessively overt or if the viral transmission vehicle isn't reaching the prospective customer set. For example, the envelope example above, applied to a pizza box, is likely ineffective; a very small percentage of the pizza box's recipients are themselves likely to be buyers of pizza boxes. Viral marketing only infects the target population.

How much should it cost per person reached? Viral marketing isn't very persuasive on a per-exposure basis. For example, few people will run out and buy envelopes based on one exposure to that printed message on the back. Viral marketing is also embedded in a product you're already producing—it's just an imprint on the envelope, in this example. So for both reasons it should cost you very little—$0 to a fraction of a cent per message (effectively the cost of the imprint on your product).

Creating Your Reputation: Implementing Word of Mouth/Becoming Viral

So how do you make your business message more infectious, and implement reputational marketing? The secret is to find ways to gain exposure on things that are simultaneously inexpensive for your company to use, related to your offering, easily transmissible, and attractive for your prospective customer base to adopt and re-transmit.

For example, consider the desktop paper products company that gave away "Post-It"® type sticky-note pads to current customers. Each pad had the company's logo, a one-line statement about their products, and a web address (URL) placed at the top of the pad. The notes were inexpensive, an example of the company's product, useful to the recipients, and were attached to documents given to other potential consumers of the desktop products. Putting logos on pens won't help you unless you're a pen manufacturer, but putting your URL on a set of free return address labels might help you if you're associated with a mail-related, address-related, or paper-related cause.

If your product itself is at all customer-exposed, you can exercise a more direct approach. Your brand should be featured prominently in at least the evaluation versions, if not the full versions of your product. Netscape and Microsoft's original web browsers included their nonremovable logo in the upper right corner of the screen—effectively doing free marketing to anyone who saw the product on anyone else's screen. Custom auto-parts manufacturers often imprint their brand prominently on the body of the part—and if the part isn't exposed, they include a window decal with the company's name in the part's package.

Incentive programs can also encourage word of mouth. For example, cards that promise a discount on your service to both parties if people introduce their friends to your product can be highly effective—as can a simple business card saying "Like us? Please give this to a friend."

Reputational marketing shouldn't be complex. Put your company's logo, one-line product description, and web URL on a piece of paper. Reduce or enlarge it to fit the size of your product. Now figure out where to attach, imprint, or embed the tag—or, like the battery makers who hand out small (battery-powered) flashlights with the battery-maker's logo on it, figure out where you could attach the tag to an inexpensive item *related* to your product, that your customers would voluntarily share with other prospective customers.

Now, produce those (inexpensive, related) logo and address-emblazoned items, and keep track of how many new customers come to you based on their exposure to those items. *If you make more in sales than the items cost you, you've started doing good marketing.*

Generating awareness via word of mouth is a cheap and easy start to marketing.

Summary: Generating awareness via word of mouth is a cheap and easy start to marketing. Just give the people with whom you interact—friends, family, suppliers, and satisfied customers—a way to tell others about you, and encourage them to do so.

▶ Put your contact information and business summary tagline on your product and small promotional items related to your business.

▶ Provide your customers with a reason and method to tell their friends about their satisfaction with your business.

▶ Be sure your choice of vehicle is a transmissible *and appropriate* one. Toys aren't useful, and pens are only good publicity for pen makers—but a transmissible item related to your business (like a notepad from a paper goods maker) may carry your message.

Alert Your Community

Everyone is part of a community. Most people are part of several. For example, simply by virtue of being an entrepreneur reading this book, you're already part of at least three communities—entrepreneurial thinkers, marketers, and readers.

Good marketers recognize the value of these communities. Drug makers advertise at medical conventions. House painters advertise on local hardware store bulletin boards. *Targeted* marketing—marketing only to people who will use your products—doesn't need to be complex when groups of potential customers have already organized and identified themselves to any interested entrepreneurs.

What's more, with the advent of Internet-based chat rooms, blogs, and other forums, *communities* (also known as *interest groups*, or *affinity groups*) have achieved sufficient size to be worthwhile marketing targets, even as the groups' interests have become more focused.

For example, in the late 1980s, there might have been only a few veterans in a town, and so they'd congregate monthly under one label, "veterans." Now, those veterans have associated with others online, and so the meetings may be more frequent (weekly, online), more granular (split up by unit or division), and *still* be larger meetings than previously held in the single-town case.

The result of this increasing granularity and focus is that entrepreneurial marketers no longer need to spend long hours doing research to hunt down the mailing addresses or phone numbers of potential buyers of your better mousetrap. A simple Internet search on "rat removal" or even "trap lovers" will produce interest groups—associations, blogs, and discussion groups—each a collection of ready-made prospects.

So where and how can you best use these groups?

Associations and Affinity Marketing

What is it? Associations are formally organized groups of people with similar interests, such as "Pest Control Professionals of Atlantis." Affinity marketing refers to the process of telling these groups about your business in a way that's meaningful to *them*—for example, emphasizing the waterproof nature of your mousetraps, and their dual-use as lobster traps, when marketing their benefits to the Atlanteans.

When should you use it? Association and affinity marketing is most appropriate when your business has a unique relationship to and benefit for a specific group—for example, drug companies marketing to doctors.

When should you not use it? Affinity marketing can do more harm than good when your business isn't appropriate to the audience—to borrow from feminist author Gloria Steinem, "marketing bicycles to fish."

How much should it cost per person reached? Affinity marketing should be relatively inexpensive *compared with other marketing efforts*. So a drug company may spend $100 per person sponsoring a dinner for a local hospital's monthly meeting of doctors, and that may seem expensive. But if for each $100 spent, the drug company will make $1,000 in sales, whereas if they'd only make $200 in sales for each $100 they spent on other marketing such as billboard advertisements, the dinner is a good investment. The cost relative to the sales they'll make will be comparably lower than the cost of other marketing to achieve similar sales.

Affinity marketing refers to the process of telling these groups about your business in a way that's meaningful to them.

Affinity marketing depends on shared interests, so the relationships can't all be cash-based. You must be able to offer unique content (presentations, research, opinions) to directly related affinity groups to be a part of them. Only then can your marketing use the created relationships.

For example, many pharmaceutical companies sponsor educational lectures for physicians. Members of a local American Medical Association chapter might receive invitations to dinner at the Four Seasons hotel, accompanied by a lecture by a known expert in a specific medical field. As part of the lecture, the sponsoring company explains how their new drug assists in the treatment of the medical condition being discussed. The pharmaceutical company assists the association—by *providing* content, as well as paying for dinner and the speaker—and in return, the company gains access to a valuable target market.

As an entrepreneur, you must understand that dinner at the Four Seasons *isn't necessary*. The secret to successful affinity marketing isn't cash; it's your skill in using the three Rs—*reduced participation*, *reciprocity*, and *referrals*.

Reduced participation means recognizing that the core of an affinity group is the affinity itself—the shared common interest. The bribe of an expensive dinner isn't a requirement if the content is relevant. For example, if your company had created an advocate out of a well-known expert, simply arranging for the expert to speak would likely have generated a large turnout at the association's meeting. If the content is sufficiently compelling or specifically targeted to the group—for example, if the content is an informational coupon explaining how the association's members uniquely benefit from your product, and offering a free trial only for them, then no personal presence at all may be needed. The group leadership may agree to disseminate the material to the group themselves. In all cases, your message may reach the target group, at a fraction of the cost of a full sponsorship.

Reciprocity refers to the fact that people will give you something if you give them something—even if the things are of significantly different value. This effect is critical to the success of the reduced participation examples above. For example, executives will fill out hour-long surveys at trade shows for a small package of golf balls. The trade is not financially equal, but it takes place nonetheless. In entrepreneurial affinity marketing, the goal is to use reciprocity to obtain the group members' time and referrals of other prospects. For example, sponsoring a pizza lunch and a presentation on how your product supports Linux, for a Linux user group (or lawn care, for a local garden club), will net your company an hour in front of a very focused target audience. If you ask the group, it will likely also bring you referrals of "other people who couldn't attend the lunch today but whom you think might be interested in this presentation—here's the opening slide, give it to them and we'll give them the rest if they e-mail this address."

Referrals then leverage the friend-to-friend relationship initially established within the affinity group. Using the prior example, referrals could be marketed to with the opening line, "Your colleague John Doe, a member of the local Linux user group of which we're also a part, has saved over $50k using NewCo. As another LUG member, we thought you might be interested in NewCo's products...."

In sum, associations are an opportunity to create a "friend" relationship through a shared common interest. If your company can legitimately claim to share the common interest, and contributes content accordingly, reciprocity will generate referrals—and you will have dramatically expanded your overall marketing reach on a shoestring budget instead of a steak dinner budget.

So start today. Call your five best customers. Ask them what associations they belong to, and whether they could refer you to those associations' meeting planners. Print up a few hundred business cards to take with you that promise a special offer, available only to members of the association printed on the front of the card, if they call or e-mail you. Offer to create a PowerPoint presentation for your customer to present at the next meeting, for which you'll bring the pizza. You have the customer relationships—now, start reaching out to the next degrees of connection, *their* relationships.

> *In sum, associations are an opportunity to create a "friend" relationship through a shared common interest.*

Blogvertising

What is it? Blogs are *web logs*—effectively, online diaries or journals kept by individuals but open to the larger Internet community to read. Blogvertising refers to sponsorship of these blogs, through advertising, product placement, or direct authorship.

When should you use it? If a community of interest in your business area exists, blogs may already exist. Sponsorship of those blogs will make the community aware of *your* business—like a gasoline company sponsoring a NASCAR commentator, the relationship is a two-way endorsement.

When should you not use it? Blog authorship or sponsorship can be a waste of money if there's no readership.

How much should it cost per person reached? Since the relationship between readership exposure and subsequent sales is tenuous at best, this should cost no more than a few cents per reader.

What's better than presenting to people with shared interests? Having an expert present to his extended affinity group—their friends—for you. Blogvertising or speaker sponsorship is an intermediate step between presenting to an association (in which you're still an outsider, albeit one with a shared interest) and creating a community (where your business *is* the shared interest).

*B*logvertising or speaker sponsorship is an intermediate step between presenting to an association and creating a community.

Like sponsoring a racing team, or a charitable group, sponsoring a speaker creates an ally. You associate your business with the attributes of the speaker (for better or worse—pick your speaker carefully), and you generate reciprocity: By supporting them, you make them comfortable endorsing you.

Of course, the strength of the endorsement and publicity will depend on the strength of the relationship. Handing a speaker (or blog author) cash in exchange for having a banner on their podium (or web site) won't foster a strong relationship. If you're lucky, the speaker will be honorable enough to refuse your offer if they don't like your product. If you're unlucky, the speaker may take your cash and then endorse a competing business in their speech or blog.

So build a relationship with your speakers. Have them use your product, and then *if* they believe in it, offer to support their efforts via cash, publicity, or free use of your product or business. Unlike your direct association marketing, the expert is already a member of the target audience: For them, speaking to the group is like your awareness generation to friends and family. Your event has much greater instant acceptance and credibility, versus being viewed as a (friendly) vendor. The awareness value they'll generate for you via endorsement to the target interest groups to whom they speak will significantly outweigh the cost to you of sponsoring them.

Created Communities and Discussion Groups

What is it? Created communities and (sponsored) discussion groups are self-created associations—associations created around your business, with you as the focal point. For example, owners of certain types of cars may enjoy trading tips on improving performance or solving problems. Recipients of a lawn care service may be avid gardeners, and share care ideas.

When should you use it? Created communities are appropriate when you have a sufficient number of customers interested in discussing your product with each other, and you can contribute sufficient new product or service information to keep conversation flowing. (Communities aren't infinitely self-perpetuating; you need to participate and provide things for them to talk about if you want to keep them alive.)

When should you not use it? Created communities will fail as a marketing vehicle if your business lacks sufficient volume of customers interested in sharing product knowledge. If you have too few users, disinterested users, or users who compete with each other and don't *want* to share information, your community won't thrive.

How much should it cost per person reached? Created communities should cost only a few dollars per member per year—effectively, the cost of sponsoring the infrastructure by which the group communicates, be that an Internet forum, mailed newsletter, or local bulletin board.

What's better than an expert presenting to his friends for you? Having friends present for you. The most personal implementation of friendship marketing is a created community. Creating a community involves *deliberately* building the equivalent of a dispersed affinity group or association of people who are willing to be advocates—even evangelists—for your company or product.

Creating communities involves making friends with your customers, then asking them to act as promoters for your company. Created communities rely heavily on reciprocity; there's not much of a friendship if the advocacy only occurs on one side of the relationship. But as in association marketing, if you can perform a service for your users, you can obtain marketing in return.

As examples, consider TiVo and Butterball. While widely differing companies, they both successfully employed the quid pro quo of reciprocity in a created community. TiVo supported online bulletin boards—discussion forums that included product hacks, criticism, and other issues. Some were of questionable value to the company. But in return for the tacit sponsorship, the discussion group members ended up eventually not only taking on a significant percentage of TiVo's customer support burden, but also assisting the company in debugging their products—and implementing new product functionality.

Similarly, Butterball Turkey created the now-famous Thanksgiving Turkey emergency phone hotline—a live, free service to provide assistance when would-be chefs encountered crises preparing the annual feast. Callers didn't need to have purchased a Butterball Turkey—the line was open to users of any brand. The result? Butterball received free positive publicity,

Creating a community involves deliberately building the equivalent of a dispersed affinity group or association of people who are willing to be advocates—even evangelists—for your company or product.

thousands of people switched brands, and competitors scrambled to create their own communities.

Created communities can be implemented on an entrepreneurial budget. People like helping other people, and rewards don't need to be cash. Create a "user group" around your product where you demonstrate solutions for customers. You'll benefit your users by providing information—and with some prompting, they'll bring in others who might benefit from the information as well. Host an online bulletin board like TiVo, awarding special icons and status to customers who help others or bring in new users. Or, like Butterball, offer a free basic support web site for your *class* of products— then follow up with the people who weren't yet users of *your* product. Using reciprocity, the goodwill you generate from people using your services can be turned into leads: Ask them to spread the word, provide an easy way for them to extend the invitation, and you can reasonably expect them to actively "tell a friend" about your service.

If your company has been delivering products for more than a year, communities will already exist. Search online for discussion groups, forums, or even domain names of the form "www.[your company name]sucks.com"— where the last in that list is arguably your best forum. Listen to these people, start participating and addressing their issues, *be* a friend—and then ask them for a favor in return. It's simple, cheap, and effective.

As physical chain letters proved long before e-mail, friend-to-friend communication works. Long ago, businesses realized that multi-level marketing, taking advantage of friendships, would also serve to sell products and services. Now, using the right attitude and current technology, it's possible to use friendships—six degrees of connection—to achieve the same reach and awareness levels provided by large multi-level-marketing networks like Tupperware, or Mary Kay, on a shoestring budget. So approach the challenge genuinely—remember that reciprocity depends on a two-way exchange relationship—and start making friends.

It's possible to use friendships—six degrees of connection—to achieve the same reach and awareness levels provided by large multi-level-marketing networks like Tupperware, or Mary Kay, on a shoestring budget.

Summary: How do you generate awareness via community? Genuinely share and support their interests as they relate to your business.

▶ At a minimum, offer relevant content: Provide information to existing groups on how your business supports their interest.

▶ Support experts in the area of interest, and they'll support you.

▶ If you have more content, create a home for the group, on the Internet or in real life.

Hang Out Your Shingle

News aside, the most *visible* aspect of awareness generation is advertising. Advertising can take many forms, from subtle product placement, where your product is briefly visible during a movie scene, to overt signage, such as the multi-story video displays of New York City's Times Square.

Yet all advertising shares a common theme: public display of overt or covert messages indicating the availability of your product or service, ideally with associated logic for why and how your intended consumer should and can purchase. The goal: Maximize their awareness and compulsion to buy.

So, is a giant video display more effective than a simple shingle at advertising *your* business? The answer depends on your business, prospective purchasers, available advertising options, and market window.

All advertising shares a common theme: public display of overt or covert messages indicating the availability of your product or service.

To make your choice the right one, follow these four steps:

▶ Understand how your customers *want* to be reached.

▶ Know your advertising options—and pick one (or more).

▶ Check your strategy against your reality.

▶ Design for success.

Advertise Appropriately: Understand How Your Customers *Want* To Be Reached

Understanding how your customers *want* to be reached is critical to your success. Why? Because:

▶ You don't have very much money to spend,

▶ You want to be noticed as much as possible,

▶ The most efficient way to reach customers is the way they prefer, and

▶ Therefore, you need to find out how they *want* to be reached.

Consider: In a world filled with perfect marketers, everyone would welcome advertising. Why? Because advertising would reach you in the way you *wanted*, listing products and services you sought to compare. Your phone would never ring at dinnertime—instead, on a day close to the day your car needed an oil change, there'd be a flyer under your windshield, or a lighted sign on your way to work advertising the necessary service. In the days of hanging out shingles, you could stand in the main street of a town and immediately see what each business had to offer.

Unfortunately, marketers aren't perfect. The result is that most customers have been flooded with advertising, often for businesses irrelevant to them, and so they've learned to psychologically block most advertising.

As an entrepreneur, your primary advertising challenge is to reach your prospective consumers' minds—then, your ads can make them aware of your business. So, how can you be sure of reaching your prospective customers? Re-check the answers to the questions you asked in Chapter 1, about your target customers' behavior. Do you understand your customers? Do you know where they get their information, in general? How do they get their information about *your* type of business?

For example, your customers may learn about new restaurants through local Yellow Pages ads, but learn about new house-painters through direct-mail offers, and learn about new car dealerships through local cable television ads. You may *choose* to attempt to access your prospective customers through a new method—but make this choice deliberately, not accidentally, as it's fraught with risk. (There's usually a reason why customers choose to learn in the way they do.)

Ask your customers how they learn about your business, and why they don't learn through other methods. Survey the customers of competing businesses. Understand how they want to be reached—or risk misplacing your advertising and spending too much.

Advertising Options

Common advertising options include physical and "virtual" media, with varying abilities to reach higher or lower numbers of people, to varying levels of impact. Consider the following:

Signs, Posters, and Billboards

▶ *What they are*: A physical surface. May be attached to your place of business, or positioned outside of where you are doing business (typical for house painting, renovation, other services), or positioned on objects or vehicles near your target audience (for example, signs or flyers on bus stops, subways, taxis, windows, and other surfaces).

- *Strengths*: Visual, brings the message close to the prospective consumer in a form that they are likely to see in a repeated way. Usually very high impression rate—based on traffic passing the sign.
- *Weaknesses*: Perceived as "low-end." (Would you buy a diamond from a company advertising in a taxi?) Inability to change message/graphics quickly means it may lose impact over time. Less targeted. (Everyone sees your subway sign, not just your intended target.)
- *Relative cost*: Inexpensive on a cost-per-impression basis.

Print Advertising (Newspaper, Magazine, Other Businesses' Catalogs)

▶ *What it is*: A paid placement of material about your company in a newspaper, magazine, catalog, or other publication.
  • *Strengths:* Reaches lots of consumers, can contain graphics such as a sign, close up so it can also contain detailed text, and with repeated impression capability (as consumers often hold on to magazines for several weeks). Also catches consumers in an information consumption mood—they're reading the publication so they will read your ad (especially if it fits into the article format).
  • *Weaknesses*: Likely still gets few impressions, and only registers peripherally on consumers' consciousness.
  • *Relative cost*: Moderate to expensive.

Radio

▶ *What it is*: Audio descriptions of your product, service, or business, mixed in with standard news and entertainment content.
  • *Strengths*: Reaches huge numbers of consumers, can convey tone (and thus implicit information about the product as well as explicit information), and has a high rate of repetition—possible to quickly convey and reinforce simple messages.
  • *Weaknesses*: Likely less specific than print—harder to target your specific target audience.
  • *Relative cost*: Moderate.

Television

▶ *What it is*: Video/audio descriptions of your product, service, or business, mixed in with standard news and entertainment content.
  • *Strengths*: Combines the reach, tone, and repetition strengths of radio with the graphic and visual strengths of signage.
  • *Weaknesses*: Like radio, limited ability to target specific audience.
  • *Relative cost*: Expensive. Best used for mass-consumer-market products in your regional area (such as house-painting, or restaurants).

Online (Internet) Graphics or Text

▶ *What it is*: Signage displayed as a graphical electronic picture, or as a text link, both as part of a web site.
  • *Strengths*: Combines the strengths of a print forum with better targeting, better repetition, interactivity, and instant response. (Would-be consumers click on a link, and are immediately directed to your web site.)
  • *Weaknesses*: See Print Advertising above.
  • *Relative cost*: Inexpensive.

Other Packaging

▶ *What it is*: Can range from labels on complementary products (for example, a label on your takeout pizza box advertising party supplies at another nearby store), to logos on small trinkets such as pens or hand-exercisers, to large-scale unique signage such as blimp or skywriter signage.

- *Strengths*: Unique signage can sometimes reach your prospective consumers when other conventional mechanisms have been overloaded (and thus consumers have been trained to ignore them).
- *Weaknesses*: Unless the item is clearly targeted, can miss your audience entirely.
- *Relative cost*: Can be quite expensive with no clear return on investment.

Checking Against Reality: Efficacy, Time, and Cost

Given your knowledge of how your customers like to receive information about your type of business, and your available options, you can choose a *preliminary* set of advertising approaches you'd like to take to maximize the awareness you generate per dollar spent.

Why preliminary? As the Rolling Stones said, "You can't always get what you want."

In a perfect world, if your customers said that they always learned about businesses like yours via television commercials, you'd immediately go out and purchase extensive commercial coverage on all major networks, and your awareness challenge would be over. Of course, if you could do that, you wouldn't be an entrepreneurial marketer, you'd be a *retired* marketer— or possibly a magician.

The facts are that advertising may or may not be available in your preferred venue or format, at an affordable price, in the time that you want it.

The facts are that advertising may or may not be available in your preferred venue or format, at an affordable price, in the time that you want it.

Moreover, since studies have proven that advertising has increased impact with increased repetition, you may need to scale back or otherwise alter your approach to change the *duration* of advertising for maximum impact.

For example, many Internet startups in 2001 discovered that a Superbowl advertisement, while reaching enormous volumes of people, had very little impact. It was like a one-minute rainstorm—a lot of people got wet, all at the same time, and then dried out very quickly. Few people remembered the Superbowl ads—the net impact on awareness (and sales) of the companies doing the advertising was minimal. Since the startup companies doing the advertising were operating on limited budgets, they couldn't repeat that impact—it was a one-shot advertising campaign.

Yet had those companies taken a different approach—perhaps putting an advertisement in the *TV Guide* on a weekly basis every week for a year, rotating the ad images but maintaining consistent messaging—the impact would have been different, like a steady drip of water instead of a short storm. The droplet approach has lower one-time impact, but over time, greater penetration.

As an entrepreneurial marketer, examine the efficacy, duration, and cost of your programs. Perhaps a print advertisement isn't your customers' primary informational source—but if it is *half* as effective as television, and you can run it *more* than twice as long or to more than twice as many people, for the same or lower cost, perhaps it's a tradeoff you want to make.

So determine your ideal advertising mix, but then modify it as needed based on actual availability. Then, create and place your ads.

Make It Happen

The last step is to create your advertisements. Different advertising media allow different types of ads. Television and radio allow an audio track. Online allows immediate response ("click through"), and should be designed to use that accordingly. Print makes more of a subconscious impression and needs to have simple, bold design. Each medium has its unique aspects. Yet there are some rules that apply to all media—so as you proceed to create your advertising for your chosen program, keep these rules in mind:

▶ Include your company name and logo.

▶ Explain what you do for consumers. (This can be done via picture, tagline, quick slogan—"Bob's Trucks: We Sell You Big Trucks.")

▶ Include a way for consumers to find you (phone number, web address, directions).

▶ Provide a *reason* for consumers to remember your name, contact information, and function—whether the reason be simply that the advertisement had positive connotations (made them smile) or ideally actually provided a unique benefit statement about your business ("Guaranteed lowest prices").

▶ Get industry benchmarks. Avoid being fleeced. Most advertising venues' actual pricing is far lower than their list pricing, especially as their end of quarter approaches (end of March, June, September, and

December) and they still have unused inventory (open ad slots).

▶ Be detailed when asking for advertising specifications from your vendor—it will save you time and money later. Important considerations include:

- Ad size, or number of text characters
- Dates ad will run
- Placement on site/in broadcast (Do you *want* your radio spot to run at 2 a.m.?)
- Payment terms (Do you pay only if you get results? How soon do you pay?)
- Legal terms (Who owns the advertisement if they create it but you pay for it?)

Bear in mind that good advertising stamps your business on your customers' brains, quickly.

Bear in mind that good advertising stamps your business on your customers' brains, quickly. Speed is of critical importance: Both the time the advertisement has in front of your prospective customer, and the size and placement of the ads—which can be graphics of various sizes, or simply standard-font linked text, or a short verbal statement on radio—conspire to minimize the window in which to communicate to the prospective customer.

Successful advertising is disruptive and concise—like the Haiku, or possibly the old Burma Shave road signs, the ads present only three or four parts:

▶ A "Grabber," or intriguing line addressing a customer problem (Problem Recognition)

▶ Value your company presents—what you do to address the problem

▶ A call to action—instructions to the customer as to how to take the next step

You don't have to have perfect ads. Customers vote with their wallets—they'll tell you what works though their purchase response to your ads (or lack thereof). So create a few ads, and do a broad but brief trial run. Show all of your ads in all of your locations. Then measure the results to see which ads and placements were most effective. Then concentrate on the more effective advertising—even as you continue to introduce new ads.

Your job will never be done—ads get stale and become effectively invisible to your prospective customers after a few exposures. So you'll always be trying new ways of communicating your message. The overall effect of advertising *is* cumulative—more ads over time produces more impact on customers. (A customer seeing the ad for the third time is more receptive than one seeing that same ad the first time.) But this is so only if the ads are fresh. So understand what's compelling about your offering, but keep finding new ways of explaining that benefit to your prospective customers.

Remember also that winners on one placement may lose on another—an ad that worked in the *New York Times* may fail in your local newspaper, and vice versa. So rotate between placements, and target your ads to the venue look and feel as well as to your prospect demographic. Don't be too wedded to a specific venue or design. If the ads don't work, try again. Engage the local business school or graphic arts school to assist you with inexpensive consulting help—and if the ads don't work, drop them as a marketing program and use other tactics.

As always, don't forget to KISS—keep it simple, stupid. If it works, repeat; if it doesn't, move on.

Summary: How can you generate awareness through advertising? Tailor your ads to your situation, and keep it simple.

> *Remember also that winners on one placement may lose on another—an ad that worked in the* New York Times *may fail in your local newspaper, and vice versa.*

- ▶ Understand how your customers learn about your business, and choose ad vehicles accordingly. A horse led to water may not drink—but it's easier to lead them to water than to slaughter.
- ▶ Balance your choice of advertising vehicle with your ability to deploy it. Are you choosing the one-big-cannon-shot approach, when lots of small bullets would work better?
- ▶ Say it simply—use concise, basic descriptions.

Get Personal and Direct

The problem with direct-mail, telemarketing, and e-mail marketing is that they have been overused and abused by bad marketers. Mention any of these three marketing techniques, and most people will wince. Such programs have been the subject of many vitriolic outpourings, jokes, and even federal legislation. They're often held up as the epitome of "sleazy marketing."

Yet these awareness-generation marketing methods remain in heavy use—because they generate sales. So what's an entrepreneurial marketer to do? How can you correctly and ethically use these techniques to effectively generate business?

Direct Mail and E-mail

What is it? Mail is a personal textual and graphical communication of your business's value directly to a prospective customer. Physical mail can carry additional promotional objects, and convey tone in its physical appearance (for example, a business using thick cream-colored paper conveys a higher-class tone than one using newsprint). E-mail is restricted to two dimensions, but can include interactive links—ways that the recipient can immediately respond to your offer, or view additional multimedia information.

When should you use it? Mail can be used throughout the purchase process, from assisting prospects in recognizing their initial need for a product, to assisting in purchasing and post-purchase follow-up. E-mail tends to be best for small bursts of information, such as reminders of near-term events, and calls to action that may be followed up without much thought by clicking a link in the e-mail. Direct physical mail can carry more information and has longer shelf-life—it stays around the target prospect's office longer—but is often more expensive to produce, less easily forwarded, and less immediate.

When should you not use it? Mail is a poor vehicle for extended discussions of your business benefits (the exception to this rule being catalogs of known "hard goods"). For complex products or businesses, mail should be used only to drive the recipients to learn more.

How much should it cost per person reached? Costs range from a few cents per person for e-mail (the spread-out cost of renting e-mail lists) to a few dollars per person for complex physical mailers (such as boxes promising a free high-end piece of computer or stereo equipment in exchange for a sales meeting).

So how do you build an effective mail program?

Set goals. Remember that mail is not in and of itself a replacement for more extensive educational collateral, such as data sheets or whitepapers. Mail is a direct-marketing vehicle—an advertising mechanism, comparable to a banner ad, just slightly longer. No one will read your mail if it's an encyclopedia. Your goal for the mail should be "get N percent of the recipients to take one action," where that action is to call you, return a reply card, or click on a web link (URL). The rest of the information you want to provide to them can be passed on once they've shown that initial interest.

Define your target audience. Given the breadth of uses, it's tempting to combine audiences, or repurpose mail. Just consider the stereotypical salutation,

E–mail tends to be best for small bursts of information, such as reminders of near-term events, and calls to action that may be followed up without much thought by clicking a link in the e-mail.

"Dear Sir or Madam," to understand why repurposed mail, insufficiently targeted, can be a poor choice. Spend the up-front time to narrowly define and segment your targets, and craft appropriate short mail for each.

Choose venues (e.g., recipient lists). Consider not only the standard demographics when buying a list ("We want to reach all SysAdmins in the *Fortune 500*.") but also likely ability to recapture, receptivity of target to mail, and specificity of mail. In other words, how likely is the person you're targeting to return to you, open the mail in the first place, or even receive the mail versus having it blocked by an administrative assistant or filter? Executives may be less likely to respond than administrators. Consider also the limitations of your venue—some rented lists go through brokers who may not handle HTML or image mail, and some lists may be more appropriate for all-text mail.

Obtain industry benchmarks. Understand the prevailing click through rates and CPM rates (cost per thousand mail names) when you plan your campaign. This will prevent both immediate overcharging by vendors (most will discount if asked), and subsequent poor overall return on your investment.

Spend time on the contract. Contracts aren't for when everything goes well—they're for when everything doesn't and everyone wants to escape liability. Read your contract and be sure it covers the following issues:

▶ *All charges*: What if you need to redo text? Images? Change fees can be high.

▶ *Liability:* What if the broker mails someone on your opt-out list (despite your presenting the list to them)? If it's a rented list, who vouches that members are "opted in" and that the vendor has the rights to rent the list?

▶ *Timing:* If deadlines are not met and they miss your launch window, does any money come back to your company? Damages as well?

Obtain and define logistical information, including schedule. Once lists have been obtained at the right price, you'll need to understand the deadlines and specifics for mailing. To whom do you deliver your mail copy? Your HTML? What's the maximum number of text characters/maximum image size in HTML? Do you need to host the images, or will they, or will images be inline? In what form should you deliver the opt-out lists (.xls, .txt, .csv) and to whom, by when? How is payment presented and by what date (i.e., Net

30)? What's the minimum turnaround time after a test mail? What's the smallest test group possible? Make sure you get a big 2'×3' wall calendar, plot other campaigns, and plot your campaign's critical dates, working backwards from the final blast. You may be surprised at how late you already are.

Implement infrastructure. Make sure you have the following in place (see also the "tools" section):

- ▶ Mail-merge program (if doing your own blast), configured to a disposable gateway (do not use your standard corporate gateway, you will be black-holed by someone every time.)
- ▶ Tracking URL (to track clicks on the call to action)
- ▶ Landing page
- ▶ Opt-out URL and automated database/list
- ▶ Sales follow-up parsing and tracking mechanism (e.g., Siebel or similar, linked either manually or automatically to your landing page)

Do the creative work. First, sit down and write the three bullet points that you want your prospect to remember. These should be in the following form:

- ▶ What problem they have that your solution addresses
- ▶ Who you are/what your solution is
- ▶ Call to action

Add your tracking URL to the last point (the call to action), and you're done! As needed, read the section above on mail design again and embellish/improve the grammar—but like a good haiku, your first concise approach may be best. Note that there's creativity in the message and the subject line. You may want to run a permutation of at least four (two contents, two subjects) and test them all on a few hundred recipients before doing the "big" mail blast to a few tens of thousands. You may spend a long time creating an appropriately short mail. It's worth it.

Run a test. Actually run several tests.

- ▶ Basic spelling, grammar, and message on someone internal to your organization who has never seen the mail before. It's surprising how many typos get through spellcheckers.
- ▶ For e-mail, SPAM-filter test (just to correct for SPAM scores).
- ▶ Format test (check how it looks in raw text, HTML, printed, etc., as appropriate).

- For e-mail, narrowband test (try downloading it over a slow modem).
- Preliminary audience test (check response from a sample group).

This series should of course be done for each permuted mail—then use the best subject/content combo. Always test. You are not your target demographic (and even if you are, you're a statistically insignificant data point). Hit a randomly selected chunk of the real audience, measure your results, and adjust.

Send it! Send your mail. If using an outsourced provider, you're done. If e-mailing through your own company servers, be sure you've used a dedicated domain (or at least gateway), and have time-sequenced your mail, or else high volumes will cause you to be automatically labeled as a "spammer" by some ISPs, with the result being that mail from your company (any mail) won't reach intended recipients (instead, it will be "black-holed," destroyed, and not resent) sometimes for periods of up to a week. There will always be some positive result from your mailer. Even if all you learn is "Gosh, we shouldn't do that again," it's a useful outcome.

Measure and supply feedback constantly. The only bad use of funds is one where the results aren't recorded (and thus nothing is learned). All marketing is an opportunity to learn about the constantly shifting characteristics of your target base and receptivity to various messages, vehicles, and execution.

Telemarketing and Paid Appointments

What is it? Telemarketing and telesales involves you, or a group you've hired, calling people on a list of prospective customers—people you believe might have interest in your product.

When should you use it? Telemarketing can be used in almost every phase of your marketing and sales cycle. It can be used to:

- obtain information or increase awareness ("Have you ever heard of this product?")
- further customer education ("May I spend a few minutes explaining why this product could save you money?")
- push to sales or trial ("Can I send you a trial version/sign you up for a trial membership? Could we set up an in-person meeting to discuss your needs further?")

When should you not use it? Telemarketing is an intrusive mechanism. It should be used carefully around privacy-conscious prospective customers,

All marketing is an opportunity to learn about the constantly shifting characteristics of your target base and receptivity to various messages, vehicles, and execution.

55

and is a poor format to complete an entire sales cycle for a complex product (few jet engines are sold exclusively via telemarketing).

How much should it cost per person reached? The cost per call or per successful contact persuaded to take action can be quite high, depending on the length of your calls, complexity of the message, and skill level (cost per hour) of the telemarketer you're using.

A good telemarketing experience for you and the people your business is calling depends on three things:

▶ Your target's willingness or desire to be called

▶ A focused interaction (don't waste their time … or yours)

▶ Benefit to both sides

So how do you create this optimal experience? Of primary importance is your target's willingness (or desire) to be called. The simplest way to obtain this permission is to solicit their phone number from them, rather than renting a list of likely prospects. For example, one very successful clothing retailer started their marketing program by leaving flyers at neighborhood businesses with "Business return code" postcards (available through the U.S. Post Office—you only pay if the card is returned), which stated simply, "we'd like to call you once a month to tell you about special, exclusive sales. You'll save at least 25%. Fill out your phone number and return the card if you *want* us to call you and invite you." Each call began by reminding the called party that this was the notification they'd requested.

If you're forced to rent a list of likely prospects—for example, "all purchasers of plumbing supplies in your area code"—follow some basic rules of etiquette. Call during business hours. Begin the call or leave voicemail that clearly identifies your purpose, and ask whether it's a good time to take five minutes (or ten, or whatever your timeframe is) of their time. For example: "My name is X, my phone number is Y, and I obtained your name from XYZ Co. as someone who wanted to be called about discounts on plumbing supplies. Are you the right person, and is this a good time to take five minutes for me to list our offerings, which will save you $1,000?" Once you've reached the right person, focus your interaction.

Before you begin calling, establish a goal and a related call script. For example, if your goal is "understand why people who visited our business once aren't returning," create a branched questionnaire that takes no more than a few minutes to complete. The first question might ask, "Have you visited us more than once?" If the answer is "yes," your next question might lead down a path of what they liked, what kept them returning, and whether they'd be willing to refer a friend. If the answer is "no," your next question might ask for a reason—and depending on their response (price, for example), have a set of preformatted responses (offering a one-time discount for them to try you again).

Lastly, be sure the experience provides value to your target person as well as to you—and mention the value up front as appropriate. Will they be privy to a special sale? A discount? A gift card? A donation to charity in their name? Entered in a drawing for a car? Listed as one of your favorite customers? They are spending their time with you; respect and compensate them for that.

If you follow the three rules above, you'll be a welcomed call—and you'll make money, too.

Summary: How can you generate awareness through direct touch? Provide short bursts of useful information in a guidedly interactive way.

- ► Remember that the medium is in part the message: Your choice of paper, graphic, send priority (overnight versus surface mail versus e-mail) and details all convey your message.

- ► Be concise and precise: Provide your information—who you are, why you're contacting them, how you got their name (optional), what benefit you'll provide, and what they should do next to realize that benefit.

- ► Respect your prospective customers' time: Ensure the interaction is of benefit to them as well as to you.

Parting Thought: It's Not Enough to Call

Telling people you exist is a great start to creating awareness. But it's not the sum total of creation of awareness. Like dropping a stone in a pond, as the ripples of your awareness campaigns spread out, they get less focused. At the edges of your campaign, there will be people who have heard about your *type* of business ("Hey, did you hear there's this great new store/service/product?") but don't immediately connect the business with *you*. You've generated awareness and possibly demand, but it's nonspecific. These people are at risk of being taken by your competitors.

So read on to the next chapter. Discover how to cast a wider net, how to be the first name people find when they think of or go looking for your *type* of solution, so that you're capturing your competitors' demand, and not the other way around.

Chapter 4

Create Awareness II: Be There to Be Seen
Putting Yourself in the Right Place at the Right Time

"When you find something, it's always in the last place you look ..."

—Anonymous

A S STATED IN THE PREVIOUS CHAPTER: IF NO ONE KNOWS YOUR BUSI-ness exists, it soon won't.

The previous chapter covered *proactive* awareness generation—awareness-generation tactics that involved actively seeking out potential users of the products or services you provide. This chapter contains techniques for *reactive* awareness generation—awareness-generation tactics that involve ensuring that potential users seeking solutions can find *you*.

Figure 4-1 outlines the different phases of proactive and reactive awareness generation.

By the end of this chapter, you will know how to gain awareness quickly and cost-effectively among customers who are *more* familiar with the type of offering your business provides, and are actively seeking solutions. If you are engaging in a business that is serving an already well-understood need—

	Customer may not even be aware they have an issue to be addressed	Customer is actively looking for a solution to their issue
Minimal Impact Reaches Many	**Start with Family:** Word of Mouth, Viral Programs	**Be News**
	Alert Your Community: Affinity Marketing, Blogvertising	**Help Them Find You:** Directories
	Hang Out Your Shingle: Advertising	**Throw a Party:** Live Events
Maximal Impact Reaches Fewer	**Get Personal and Direct:** Mail, Telemarketing	**Build Instant Credibility:** Partnering and Co-marketing

Figure 4-1. Reactive and proactive awareness generation (same idea as Figure 3-1)

for example, you're providing another taxi service in a city where taxis are used—you should use these types of tactics.

This chapter will show you how to:

▶ **Be news:** Generate awareness via public relations/press, by being amusing, quotable, or new.

▶ **Help them find you:** Generate awareness via availability, in online or physical directories.

▶ **Throw a party—connect live:** Generate awareness via personal interaction, through webinars and seminars.

▶ **Build instant credibility and reach (just add friends):** Generate awareness via partnerships, allying with bigger players.

As was the case with the last chapter, these are tactics any entrepreneur can use, without a large budget or the assistance of a marketing agency.

Be News

The saying "No news is good news" does *not* apply to your business. *News*, by definition, is the spread of information and *awareness*. The big news providers will spread information and awareness to more people than you can possibly reach by spending your entrepreneurial marketing budget on advertising.

So for you, "*all* news is good news"—and the good news is that it's easy to *be* news. Media providers need you as much as you need them. Magazines, newspapers, journals, and other periodicals survive on *content* as well as advertising. So why pay for advertising when you can "be contented"—when you can achieve the same or better results with content?

It's true: You can reach more people, for less money, and more effectively by *being* news instead of paying for advertising; by generating content that the news media will *want* to spread for you. The secret is in giving them *usable* content. You wouldn't gift your dinner party host with a bunch of grapes and a bucket, you'd give them a bottle of wine. Similarly, you need to prepare your content for the media before asking them to trade for exposure.

To be valuable to the media, news must be *interesting* information—information that people will read, listen to, seek out, and forward to others. Yet when attempting to provide news, via direct or media-related communication, too often marketing and sales managers remember the "information" part but forget the "interesting" part.

What's interesting? Things that entertain you or change your life are interesting.

The fact that your latest product was released is not interesting to anyone but you. It's not news. It's information, but it's boring information, which doesn't necessarily change anyone else's life.

In contrast, what your product does *for* people may be news. If your product creates radical change for a well-known company, that's news. If you are an interesting person, able to comment in an entertaining or expert way on an industry or area of current interest, you're news. In short, there are at least three ways to be ready-to-use news:

- ▶ Be an expert.
- ▶ Be a new, useful discovery: Change the way something is done, making it cheaper/easier/faster.
- ▶ Be entertaining.

Be An Expert

What is it? News citing you or your business as an authority is expert news.

When should you use it? Being cited as an expert will improve your business' credibility under almost any circumstances.

When should you not use it? If you wish to avoid being noticed by large competitors, or if the news source citing you would remove credibility (e.g., tabloid news citing you on a serious topic), avoid being quoted.

How much should it cost per person reached? The target audience reached by

You can reach more people, for less money, and more effectively by being news instead of paying for advertising.

this type of news article is an excellent one—and so it's worth spending significant time and financial resources to establish yourself as an expert. With the cost amortized—spread out—over the number of potential customers who will read about you as an expert, the investment is still inexpensive on a per-person basis.

As Harold Ross of the *New Yorker* said, "If you can't be funny, be interesting." Being an expert is another way to make yourself attractive to the media. For example, consider Roger Salquist. Roger was the CEO of Calgene, one of the companies that pioneered the creation of genetically engineered food. Roger was also an exceptional producer of sayings, quips, and *bons mots*. Knowing this, Roger made an effort to meet and mingle with journalists at industry events, and was always ready with an interesting quotable comment on current industry happenings. The result? Roger soon became the de facto "color commentary" added to any article on the industry. Soon, no reputable article was without a quotation from him—and they all mentioned his position as CEO of Calgene. Roger had become the media-appointed industry expert.

As Roger demonstrated, it's relatively easy and inexpensive to be an expert, or at least look like one. Expertise can be self-created and self-fulfilling. For example, one investment banking analyst released a poster in the late 1990s, describing "The Internet" from an architectural standpoint. Within a few months, the poster was visible in the cubicles and halls of almost every company in Silicon Valley—and the analyst was considered the expert in the category.

So how did he do it? The analyst had simply figured out about what his customers wanted to hear, sent out solicitation e-mails with the (free) poster offer, and recorded the subsequent demand. Once media companies were shown the apparent popularity of the poster—the "proof" of market demand for his expertise—they were willing to provide coverage of the story, which in turn fueled further demand. Soon, the analyst's "expertise," real or created, was well established.

The key tactic for you to use in turning yourself into a publicly acknowledged expert is the creation and publicity of interesting content, in an inexpensive way. Good "starter" content includes research reports or opinion papers. Research can be inexpensive—just do an online survey of your customers and aggregate the data. Opinions are even less expensive—go visit your customers, listen to what they say to you, and write up your memories and opinions. Then be sure that several media outlets' fax numbers and

The key tactic for you to use in turning yourself into a publicly acknowledged expert is the creation and publicity of interesting content, in an inexpensive way.

e-mail addresses are on the recipient list for your *controversial* study or paper and associated press release.

Seem too simple? Bear in mind that companies pay tens of thousands of dollars to research groups like Forrester for exactly this type of information. Anyone can be an expert—and the benefit is that not only will your media-designated expertise drive awareness of your company among the right prospective customers, but it will also allow you to influence that audience's criteria for subsequent purchases. After all, if the expert opinion in the market is that certain features are critical aspects of a great product, why would any purchaser risk their job by opposing the expert?

Be A New, Useful Discovery

What is it? News related to "new discoveries" can be presented as a scientific or consumer article, or product review.

When should you use it? If your business or product is significantly better than that of the competition, or if you can define the evaluation criteria such that you score better than they do on those aspects, these articles will generate good publicity.

When should you not use it? If you "lose" a competitive review against a competing business or product (for example, consider a restaurant or performance review that pans you), you've generated negative awareness.

How much should it cost per person reached? The cost should be minimal—effectively, the cost of creating the review—but the prior comments on "being an expert" also apply.

What's a new, useful discovery? Where a product or service is concerned, a new useful discovery is either a *new solution* to an existing problem, or a *new improvement* to an existing solution. For example, the ultrasonic device to drive away rodents was a *new solution*; the have-a-heart no-kill trap was an *improvement* on the old snap trap. Both were better mousetraps. Both put the "new" in "news."

New solutions reach the media in the form of product reviews. Standalone or competitive reviews of your product are useful both to the media and to you because they're a win-win-win situation. The reviews serve your needs, the media's needs, and the consumer's needs. The media provider knows the reviews will provide compelling content, consumers get new information, and you get free positive media exposure.

Consider: Have you ever turned down a copy of a consumer review on a product you're thinking of buying? After reading those reviews, how often did you purchase one of the top-ranked products? If you're still not convinced that product reviews are news, just think about how often new cars are reviewed in your local paper. Now, go call the relevant journals for your industry and offer to participate in some reviews—or even hire an independent reviewer to do the reviews yourself.

New improvements to existing solutions are harder to position for the media, but if correctly positioned, can be featured more prominently, with correspondingly greater impact on your sales funnel. Improvement news reflects the *results* produced by your product. Documentation of these improvements usually takes the form of a customer success story, memorable quotation, or report. For example, if your company saved a customer significant amounts of money, that's news. It's even better news when produced as a full-color return on investment (ROI) report with charts and graphs showing how much money the company saved or made relative to what they spent on your product, or as an anecdote with quotes from that company.

Why does this information qualify as news? It appeals to prospective customers, both yours and the media's. Specifically, your would-be prospects want to make their businesses into industry-leading companies. Like high school students looking at movie stars in magazines to understand fashion trends, these prospective customers read industry journals seeking guidance, looking for best practices of leading companies, hoping to find tips on becoming one. If you can be the supplier to an industry-leading company—providing a success story or unusual change situation—you're the equivalent of the fashion designer for the movie star. You'll be news for your target audience, which in turn will drive publication sales, and the associated media coverage will provide compelling awareness generation to your target audience. All for free.

So how can you get your company noticed by the media for a new and useful discovery? Make reporters' lives easy. Write the story *for* the media. For example, in the product review situation, provide a "Reviewer's Guide." This document, illustrated with diagrams and photographs as appropriate, should include step-by-step instructions for using your product—the product that you have already installed and set up for the reviewer. Write the document so that any person with even the slightest familiarity with the industry could operate your product and see evidence of the benefits you describe. Include a customer success story for context. This is your chance to set the agenda for comparison. So clearly explain why the functionality demonstrated is superior to any other company's solution. Distribute the guide in hardcopy and electronic formats, with the photos in formats easily convertible to print by the reviewers. Make your reviewer's life easy—they'll reward you for it.

Similarly, in the customer case, create a written "customer success story." When choosing your customer, balance how well known they are and how good their story is against how easy it will be to get them to appear in the media. Write down what they did with your product. Obtain quotations and any charts they used internally to convince their investors or executive staff that the use of your product was a success—how much money or time they saved, how much of a competitive advantage they gained. If possible, get their legal department to allow you to use their name and brand publicly. If you encounter resistance, find the highest-ranking executive in the company who's aware of the product results, and offer them the publicity if they can clear the legal hurdles. Everyone wants to be a star.

In both cases, product review and customer success story, remember: News isn't about you. It's about the impact of your product. To paraphrase John F. Kennedy, "Ask not what your customers can do for you, but what you and your product can do for your customers... and the media."

Be Entertaining

What is it? News related to celebrity and nonbusiness "distractions" is entertainment.

When should you use it? If your business has advantages over competitors, and is suffering from lack of awareness *only*, any publicity could be useful.

When should you not use it? Entertainment is the least-targeted form of publicity and awareness, likely reaching very few of your target audience, but certainly alerting competitors.

How much should it cost per person reached? The cost is restricted to the cost of obtaining celebrity status—but should be restricted, due to the aforementioned lack of specificity.

The easiest and lowest-risk corporate approach to entertainment is to create celebrity.

Entertainment is a multi-billion-dollar business, and celebrity stories, controversy, and distractions all make good entertainment content. The easiest and lowest-risk corporate approach to entertainment is to create celebrity. For example, as well as being an extremely successful CEO, Larry Ellison provides good entertainment. He has been featured in the news for his mansion, his flying habits, his yacht racing, and his personal life. In many ways, his public persona is more rock star than CEO. Bill Gates leverages similar exposure through philanthropic giving. Sir Richard Branson, of Virgin, and real-estate magnate Donald Trump provide similar examples of businesspeople leveraging celebrity. While the value of personal qualities and image association can be debated (aggressive, adventuresome, and sports-loving are appealing attributes in a company; litigious, misogynistic, and snide aren't), the press exposure associated with celebrity is free and extensive.

Controversy and distractions are also inexpensive to create. Smaller companies, and even individuals—for example, bloggers—have become news by creating popular product-related games, unique items or events, or simply well-written or controversial punditry, then posting it on the Internet. For example, the Drudge Report went from web page rant to CNN fodder. Rathergate was a story broken by a blog, not a mainstream publication. As Andy Warhol said, "In the future, everyone will be world-famous for fifteen minutes"—and his future is now.

So how can you be entertaining on a startup budget? Leverage controversy, celebrity, and distraction. Rock bands do this by trashing hotel rooms; entrepreneurial marketing managers do this in less expensive, more productive ways. For example:

- ▶ Contribute to public forums or newsgroups. Broadcast.com founder Mark Cuban did this for several hours each week, and was soon being quoted in mainstream media.

- ▶ Issue press releases with outrageous commentary, or featuring good deeds. "Founder says if the CIA had been using their product, 9/11 would never have happened." "Whole company shaves heads in solidarity with cancer patient, but is confident their hair-growth product will assist in recovery."

- ▶ Create a public hero. Choose someone with wit, charm, presence, and great speaking ability—and start booking them into appropriate forums to talk about your product and company. This person can be an officer, like Jerry Yang at Yahoo, or Frank Purdue and Purdue Chicken, or Dave Thomas of Wendy's, or just a staff member turned evangelist, like Guy Kawasaki at Apple.

- ▶ Create public distraction. Bessemer Venture Partners posted an anti-portfolio—a humorous commentary on the VC business—on their site, which attracted more traffic than many of their other pages. Northwest Airlines created a branded trivia game that could be passed around via e-mail. Avon created a web site where they donated ten cents to a breast-cancer awareness program for every visitor the page received.

While not useful for later-stage product education marketing or targeting, free media should at least boost name and brand awareness. If consistently coupled with the right tagline or benefits statement ("Larry Ellison, CEO of Oracle, *the world's leading relational database company*"), news can effectively supplant basic advertisements, drive prospective customers to your company, and add a substantial volume of leads to the beginning of the sales funnel.

Summary: How do you generate awareness via news media? Provide content (news).

▶ Be an expert. Market your expertise, and it will become a reality.

▶ Be a new, useful discovery. Write the story for the reviewer.

▶ Be entertaining. Make use of controversy, celebrity, and distraction.

Help Them Find You

A little narcissism isn't a bad thing when trying to generate awareness. Too many *insufficiently* self-centered entrepreneurial marketers spend all their time trying to reach target customers. Narcissists, on the other hand, say simply, "how can all the prospects who want business services like mine find *me*?"

Your easiest sales will come from prospective customers who are already far along in the purchase process, who are actively seeking solutions. In fact, if you've executed well on your other awareness-generation techniques, these customers may even know your name already. Yet if you aren't an easy and immediate result of their search, you'll miss the sale.

Awareness, therefore, should ensure your customers' brain contains both *content* and *connection* information—knowledge of your business and the way your customer connects with your business.

You need to be close to heart *and* close to hand. But the days when "close to hand" meant solely "phone number listed in the Yellow Pages" are long gone. Your prospective customers have innumerable choices when it comes to *searching* for information—so when planning awareness generation, you must plan *availability* as well.

Availability means being findable, in several ways:

- ▶ Offline
- ▶ Online
- ▶ Paid or free

Offline Contact Mechanisms: Phone Books and Directory Assistance

What is it? Listings of businesses' phone numbers and addresses.

When should you use it? Always. The question is "in how many directories should my business be listed?" Use more directories if your business is more phone-oriented (for example, take-out restaurants), and use more focused directories if your business is more specialized (for example, an industry list of all suppliers of specialty plumbing contractor tools).

When should you not use it? If your business is more dependent on foot traffic (for example, a pushcart business or local retail shop) or is otherwise less phone-dependent (for example, an online auction or financial business), you may not need or want to widely publicize your phone number.

How much should it cost per person reached? The cost should be low to moderate, depending on the criticality of the directory listing to your business. Phone-dependent businesses should view directories as a primary point of marketing, and spend on larger placement in the directory accordingly.

When trying to contact a business, most people's first instinct is to reach for the telephone.

But if they don't remember your phone number, what happens? They consult a *directory*.

Directories aren't just the local phone company's Yellow Pages. Directories include multiple types of physical *and* electronic guides. Specifically, they include:

- ▶ **Physical phone books.** These can be regional or national, alphabetic or by type of business (white pages or Yellow Pages). These are usually produced by at least one local phone company—and often several phone companies competing in the region. Additionally, there are often specialized directories—for example, a plumbing industry group may release a list of all certified plumbing supply stores.
- ▶ **Directory assistance.** These "1-area code-555-1212" or "411" telephone numbers provide semi-automated or live operator assistance to look up the

same phone numbers. Again, bear in mind that several phone companies may provide service in a given area (cellular and land-line, for example).

Being available by phone means more than simply having a phone number listed in a single directory. Availability means you have a directory *presence*—ideally, a graphically visible one. If your business name is memorable, simply having multiple white-pages listings or directory assistance may be sufficient, but if you are one of many similar businesses, you should follow the advertising and signage principles mentioned earlier and take out a sizeable graphical advertisement.

Be sure to balance cost and result! Most people only use one directory to obtain their information—but you don't know which one. Depending on your audience, that directory may be the industry listing or the local Yellow Pages (from a specific phone company). Do a "trial run" over a few months where you seed a similar listing in a wide array of likely directories—then measure your results by asking your customers where they found you, or simply listing a different phone number in each directory. Then invest more in the directories that work.

Online: The Internet

What is it? Listings of businesses' e-mail addresses and web pages (and possibly also phone numbers and addresses) on centralized, electronically searchable, rapidly updated web sites.

When should you use it? Whenever it's free. If you need to pay for the electronic listing, understand what percentage of your purchasers will find you on that listing site versus through alternative means.

When should you not use it? If your business is not committed to having an Internet web presence—if you don't have a web site, don't check your e-mail at least twice a day, and don't have customers who look for you via Internet search—it's not worth expending resources to be listed.

How much should it cost per person reached? The cost should be between nothing and a few dollars per person, based on the criticality of reaching the audience. If your customers all find you via web searches, and there are several businesses like yours competing for the same search terms, leasing those keywords can be expensive.

The electronic equivalent of the physical directories exists on the Internet, too—but it is obviated by the ability to do a "random access" search. When your prospects feel the need of your business's services, they're no longer constrained to the few listings in the local directory—they can obtain thousands of listings instantly by visiting an Internet *search site*.

Of course, for local services (restaurants, dry cleaning, lawn care) Internet searches may provide less comprehensive coverage than would physical directories—so you'll need to be listed in both—but for sheer volume of people exposed to your product, it's difficult to beat being a top listing on an Internet search site or relevant online industry directory (for example, Google and Yahoo, respectively).

Try to think like your customer. What search terms would they use to describe your business? Be sure your web site features those words, spelled in both the correct and incorrect forms and abbreviations, and that others link to your web site as a resource for those terms. (Ask your colleagues and friends to link their sites to yours.) Check the results by using the search sites themselves—all provide free tools that will generate estimates of probable numbers of impressions on specific words you enter. Still need to be more visible? Lease the critical terms from the search engine—so that when people enter the name of your competitor on Google, for example, your business appears as a top result.

As you did with physical directories, monitor your results, and spend more being visible where your customers seem to find you. Unlike the physical world, there is a reinforcement effect: The more popular you are in an Internet search, the more likely you are to appear as a result in subsequent searches—and thus become more popular. This effect is as though the more people who responded to your Yellow Pages ad, the bigger that ad became. So given the reinforcement effect, it may be worth paying for initial "popularity" (top ranking) in search results, just to start the cycle.

Paid or Free?

Do you need to pay for keywords, Yellow Pages, or other listings? In the physical world, if your other awareness activities are sufficient to broadcast a sufficiently memorable contact phone number, you may not need to spend the extra money for a directory listing. In Northern California, for example, there's a Bank of America on every corner, and their advertising touted "1-800-The-BofA" as their phone number—with the result that they didn't need the additional Yellow Pages "signage."

Similarly, online, few people trying to find Microsoft Corporation bother typing "Microsoft" into a search engine—they visit Microsoft's web site directly. The few who do type in a related product query, such as "office software," or "windows," are immediately overwhelmed with information about Microsoft from unsponsored search results. Microsoft doesn't need to pay for those keywords because they're already the de facto destination.

The answer, therefore, to the question "do you need to pay for listings" is based on your success with other media. If you've saturated your prospective audience's perceptions, so that your business has become synonymous with the solution to them (for example, "I have to Xerox this document," or "I need to FedEx this package"), you may not need the paid placement. But if you're sufficiently obscure *or* in a very competitive space (for example, you're one of 20 pizza parlors, or manufacturers of custom motorcycle tailpipes in the area), you may benefit from the increased listing exposure: Prospects may make their purchase *destination* decision *after* making their purchase decision.

Seven Things You Must Do To Be Easily Findable

So how can you ensure you're close to hand when a purchaser, their mind set on buying a solution to their problem, reaches for his phone and directory (or computer and Internet search site)?

- ▶ *Be listed:* Do your research to understand what directories exist, and test listings in each.
- ▶ *Be categorized correctly*: If you're a dining establishment, you should be categorized under restaurants and take-out, not "industrial catering"—and be sure your French café doesn't appear among the Thai listings.
- ▶ *Be visible*: If there are 1,000 listings in the physical Yellow Pages, you'll be invisible unless you're at least a 1-inch ad in line with the listings, or a quarter-page ad on the page border.
- ▶ *Be first:* In physical Yellow Pages, companies would begin their names with AAA to appear first. Online, only the first three search results are considered by consumers—so pay what it costs to be there.
- ▶ *Be available*: People call you to speak to a live human being. Don't have a phone menu of more than three options—where one is "Directions and Hours," and one is "Talk to a live person." Then set up your phone to page you or follow you (e.g., ring your cellular phone or extensions).
- ▶ *Be memorable:* "1-800-The-BofA" is much easier to remember than 843-2632—and BofA.com is easier than BankOfAmerica.com (though both work).
- ▶ *Be reliable:* Cellular phone numbers are lifetime numbers—they can follow you even as you switch locations and carriers, and can be forwarded to

land lines. Why risk annoying your customers by switching phone numbers? Get one phone number, one e-mail address, and stick with them.

In brief, be as close to your customers' hand as to their heart—and be very close to both.

Summary: How can you generate awareness through availability? Ensure that you are placed prominently in directories, so that you show up as the answer to customers' searches, whether electronic or physical (visual).

▶ Choose the right directories, physical or electronic, general or industry-specific.

▶ Be visible. Be sure your listing is visible, is placed in the right category, and is presented when customers search for your type of business or solution.

▶ Pay for placement as necessary, based on the value of the customers you'll capture.

Join the Party: Live Events

As advertising (in the prior chapter) is to directory listings (in this chapter), so is affinity group marketing to live event marketing. In both pairs, the tactic in the prior chapter involved you finding and going out to meet your prospective customers; the parallel tactic in this chapter involves making it easy for would-be customers who are already searching for a solution to find you.

So why participate in a live event, instead of only using mass-market advertising such as billboards and banners? On initial consideration, it may not seem to make sense. After all, exhibiting at a trade show or local fair costs you quite a lot of money. You could certainly reach more people with your message if that money was spent on advertising or mail. But if your business is complex, requiring more customized explanation (what can your tax planning service do for this specific client); depends on your personality for differentiation (such as a performance business); or benefits from trial (all bakeries may look the same in the Yellow Pages, but once they taste your wares customers are yours for life), then you may actually create more true awareness (becoming resident in prospective customers' consiousness versus simply making a brief impression) by participating in a live event, such as:

▶ Conference call;

▶ Webinar; or

▶ Trade show, seminar, or other face-to-face presentation event.

Conference Call

What is it? A conference call allows you to present your business as part of a multi-person phone call, where other listeners may be allowed to ask questions, or "sign in" and "drop off" the phone call as they choose during the course of your presentation.

When should you use it? If you can find a conference call being presented by a known industry analyst, partner, or other luminary who will draw a crowd, a conference call allows you to explain your product or business with more tone, interactivity, and customization for your audience than an ad.

When should you not use it? Conference calls are not awareness-generating for you if you're the one setting up the call—in that situation, you need to generate awareness of the call itself (using the mechanisms described earlier in this chapter), and the call serves as an attraction to capture contacts (see next chapter). You won't necessarily obtain any new awareness.

How much should it cost per person reached? Conference calls can be inexpensive, at a few cents per minute per listener, or quite expensive, at more than a dollar per minute per user.

As was the case with the affinity groups discussed in the last chapter, conference calls or web-based streaming broadcasts can serve as an effective one-to-many marketing technique. Unlike discussion groups, conference calls are considered less interactive. They're more formal, one-way presentations. As such, etiquette allows more open "selling" of your products in calls than in discussion groups. Also, because audio is used instead of typed web pages or e-mail, nuances of tone in presentation may be better preserved on the conference call. Yet audience feedback may be more restricted, less engaged, and with a smaller reach than is the case with discussion groups, as calls don't allow asynchronous participation. This isn't all bad: Calls may consequently be even more "prepared" or scripted than an online discussion, as long as the call is moderated or set to "broadcast only" so listeners can't interrupt.

So how can you do a conference call on an entrepreneurial budget? Start by finding a partner to sponsor it, and making the call a streaming Internet audio broadcast instead of an actual telephone call. Not only will this make the event less expensive, but it will also open up your event to international participation. Streaming server software is available for free, and bandwidth is cheap, compared to the cost of telephone connections, which can easily cost 50 cents or more per minute per line. Offer your audience the opportunity to provide concurrent feedback via Internet chat clients such as "instant messenger," or via a non-toll-free telephone call-in number, like a radio show. Host the call, and then post the recording on your site for playback. It's simple. Of course, "broadcast only" further disengages the audience, especially given a lack of visual materials, so making the call interactive but moderated is preferable.

Again, it is critical to find an existing planned call with an audience that matches your target customer profile, instead of creating the event yourself, if you are using the call to introduce yourself and create awareness in a new audience. (The exception in this case is if a partner will publicize the event to a new audience.)

Webinars

What is it? Webinars combine audio (delivered via a phone line or streamed from a computer-attached microphone over the Internet) with Internet-delivered PowerPoint or video presentations, so that many people can watch and listen to your live presentation on their computer screens, while sitting at their desk, rather than having to attend a live seminar.

When should you use it? Webinars are an excellent method for providing complex information to an already-interested audience of people, in a way that doesn't take too much time or effort on their part.

When should you not use it? Webinars aren't as engaging as a live presentation, and require the audience to be interested already—in this sense, they don't generate awareness per se, but rather provide a method of deepening business understanding.

How much should it cost per person reached? Webinar hosting providers typically charge a few thousand dollars to host webinars (and replays) for three to six months.

Webinars combine the best aspects of a conference call and a seminar—they have the convenience, low cost, and reach of a conference call, but the visual aspects of a seminar. You present a primary slideshow or live-demonstration presentation, but can easily allow the audience to ask questions or even chat among themselves via a "chat window" interface. This can allow you to better guide the direction of the "conversation" via selective response and selective sharing of chat questions with the audience.

Like audio-only conference calls or broadcasts, webinars can be hosted on an extremely small budget. Software exists for streaming PowerPoint, and there are webinar companies that will charge only a few thousand dollars for a quarterly contract to host unlimited webinar sessions. The only equipment you need is your computer, a broadband (i.e., not dial-up modem) Internet connection, and an inexpensive headset, available at any local electronics store. Of course, as was the case with the audio conference call, you'll re-use your webinar by recording it and making it available for playback on your web site.

So don't be shy—remember, if you need to, you can write your entire script down and simply read your webinar presentation. No one can see you. But a combination of voice and visuals provides much more powerful marketing than either one used separately. With a strong presentation and an interactive chat window for users to ask questions and be engaged, you can't lose.

Seminars and Shows

What is it? Live events can range from formal industry trade shows in conference centers to casual downtown street fairs. The commonality is the opportunity to set up a table and expose potential customers (event visitors, drawn by the theme of the event) to your business.

When should you use it? If your product or business is complex, requiring more customized explanation; depends on your personality for differentiation (such as a performance business; or benefits from trial, *and* the event theme is consistent with your business (don't advertise dog products at a cat show), then a live event is a good option.

When should you not use it? If your product is sufficiently simple or so complex that advertising and online exposure can convey its benefits, live event presence may not be needed. When was the last time you saw a Cheerios booth at a local street fair, versus the booth of a local bakery or restaurant?

How much should it cost per person reached? Given the cost of space, materials, and time off, live events can be quite expensive.

From patent medicines to Tupperware parties to infomercials, almost every industry in the last 150 years has used live presentations to sell its products. Whether you're simply a speaker at a live event, or a full exhibitor, a live event brings together your prospective purchasers and your company's staff for a live presentation or set of presentations about your company's product or service offerings. These events range from small, more interactive "executive forums" or "customer councils" to large, several hundred- to thousand-person multi-track workshops, booths, or product presentations. Live events offer a compelling format for extended product discussions, demonstrations, and situations where peer pressure and interactivity can assist you in making the sale.

A good presentation should be personal and dynamic. You (and the other event exhibitors) are the reason that attendees have taken time out of their busy work schedule. They've come to see a live presentation instead of reading your web site or watching a webinar because you offered them a compelling reason to attend. So be sure to meet and exceed their expectations, in an entertaining, educational way that makes use of the in-person, interactive nature of the forum.

The following checklist should provide some guidance in planning your event.

- ▶ **Choose a relevant topic:** The larger the audience you're attempting to lure to hear your pitch, and the earlier stage that audience is in the purchase process, the more related to currently topical issues your seminar must be. For example, after the 9/11 terrorist attacks, "Disaster Recovery and Backup" was an extremely popular seminar topic in all industries. Taking a contrarian's view can also sometimes help your seminar stand out from the crowd. For example, challenging the status quo in the wake of 9/11 by arguing that preparedness is futile would certainly have gotten attention. But even a contrarian's view depends on its relation to current events.

- ▶ **Choose and confirm speakers:** Find speakers appropriate to your event. It's critical that the speakers be great presenters, knowledgeable about your company and product, appropriate to the audience to which they'll be presenting, and available when you need them to present. If attempting to involve customers to speak on your behalf at your event, start the recruitment process early in your event planning. Not only are customers' schedules full, but they will usually need to obtain managerial and legal approval within their own companies—which can take quite a while, and is by no means assured. Be sure to offer appropriate customer incentive (free product, fame). Have backup plans in case the customer or your speaker is unable to attend the event.

- ▶ **Choose and schedule venues:** Every event happens somewhere—but without somewhere to happen, yours may not. Don't wait until the last minute; book hotels or conference centers early and involve your local sales representatives to find the perfect locale. When booking, work with the dedicated venue contact and discuss your list of required items with them. Understand what costs will accrue, and negotiate. Never pay list price. Read the fine print on your contract—you need to know what costs you will incur if you cancel or reschedule your event.

▶ **Obtain other staff:** If your event is sufficiently large, you may need assistance in handling registration and check-in on site. Your local sales representatives should be free to mingle with their prospects and customers—they shouldn't be required to staff a table—so consider hiring local help. Even a single-day temp worker is acceptable as long as you remember to bring a company shirt for them to ensure that they're appropriately dressed. If needed, you can enlist the help of a national staffing company with a large employee network that specializes in staffing local events.

▶ **Arrange presenter travel plans:** Always have presenters stay at the venue that will host the presentation. This enables presenters to examine their presentation room, take delivery of their collateral boxes, check for appropriate hotel signage, and avoid commute uncertainty the next day. Presenters should arrange travel to arrive at the hotel by five p.m. on the day before the event. This ensures flexibility in case of delay, as well as giving the presenter time to practice, troubleshoot, relax, and get a good night's sleep before the event. Be sure that both the corporate presenter and associated technical presenter have both hardcopy and softcopy versions of all critical materials (presentation, handout) for redundancy in case of logistical problems. Make sure your presenters also have a USB flash-drive (a small storage device that plugs into the USB port on a computer) on hand to transfer materials between computers if needed.

▶ **Pack the collateral boxes:** Start early, outsource printing of materials to be distributed, and be sure location-specific items are correctly assigned to location-specific boxes.

Overall, the best seminars are those that follow commonsense "party planning" logic. Make your guests feel comfortable and at home. It's impossible to have too much good food. It's always better to have too small, warm, and bright a room than too large, cold, and dark a room—and of course, if the seminar *feels* professional and successful, it *is* professional and successful.

Build Instant Credibility (and Reach), Just Add Friends

Reputations are like perfume; they rub off onto nearby people. Also like perfume, your business' reputation (and ability to reach others) can be improved or degraded by the company you keep. Pick the right partners and marketing allies, and you'll come out smelling like a rose—pick the wrong ones, and you just stink.

As established in the first section of the chapter, in an information-rich environment, you *and everyone you know* depend on friends and family to help filter input—it's well established that consumers are more receptive to a message when it's associated with a "known good" source.

That source doesn't have to be an individual. It can be a publication, or a product they already know and trust. For example, a favorable review in a consumer magazine or newspaper can positively influence sales—as can having your business represented by a known high-quality provider. Which would you rather have, the generic toaster-cake or Pop-Tarts™ with real Smuckers™ jam?

So if you aren't already a known entity, go find a great partner who is established in the marketplace, offer them something of value, and hope their scent rubs off. Work with them to achieve:

▶ Marketing alliances

▶ Bundling

▶ Co-branding

Marketing Alliances

What is it? A marketing alliance involves featuring both businesses in either's marketing or sales channels. For example, a local electronics store and cellular phone store might feature each other's products, or provide joint coupons.

When should you use it? If each partner brings something to the party, it's a good alliance. For example, if an ice cream store is known for its birthday cakes, but has no delivery service, and a local pizza shop has a delivery service and is trying to break into the birthday party catering business, the two can effectively combine marketing and delivery options.

When should you not use it? If the services are competitive or unrelated, the match will be poor. Two identical dry-cleaning businesses, for example, might not wish to ally, even if one currently has a better delivery service and the other has better scheduling. Similarly, a travel service and a local furniture store might serve the same type of customers, but are such unrelated businesses that co-marketing wouldn't make sense.

How much should it cost per person reached? Co-marketing should cost less than standalone marketing—as you and a partner are now sharing costs.

Ideally an alliance is a partnership that your customers have already been asking for, or even creating for you. So building the alliance should be as simple as asking your customers who they use with you, then doing some math, and talking to your would-be partner.

For example, Safeway stores observed that people would often stop at nearby banks on their way go shopping, then get a cup of coffee, and then do their grocery shopping. Safeway partnered with Wells Fargo (among other banks) and Starbucks, giving them space in the Safeway grocery stores, in exchange for rent and co-marketing (where the two other chains featured Safeway advertising in their mailers). Safeway lacked new ways to advertise to high-value customers; Wells Fargo and Starbucks lacked ways to put their products conveniently in front of customers. The partnership benefited all three companies.

So observe your customers. Is there another business they visit just prior to or after yours? Are there brand-name products they use in their home that are related to your business? Assess how much money they're spending on those products, *and the competitors of those products*—then approach that other business with your financial calculations of customer spending, and offer to partner. Point out that by co-promoting their business with you, or stocking their product with you (in exchange for financial considerations) they can have yet another sales outlet, giving them more customers and their competitors fewer customers. They should eagerly join forces with you.

Bundling

What is it? Bundling is actually shipping your product in the same package as that of a partner.

When should you use it? If the products are used together, bundling makes sense as a convenience for your customer (as well as a way to get ahead of a competitor).

When should you not use it? If the products are unrelated, one of the two or more in the bundle will be viewed as a nuisance and thrown out at best—at worst, an unbundled competing product will be preferred by the customers.

How much should it cost per person reached? Bundling should lower individual packaging costs, and therefore cost less overall.

In the mid-1990s most personal computers came with Microsoft Windows installed as an operating system, and AOL Internet software installed as an application. Did this advantage Microsoft and AOL over other operating system and Internet browsing companies? Absolutely—it took extra effort and money for consumers to choose and install different software.

As an entrepreneur, you should ask yourself how your product or business is used. No product or service is too basic to be bundled—so think big. Are you in the specialty foods business, and your customers tell you they use your chutney on steak? Work with a grocer to include a small pack of chutney inside every shrink-wrapped package of steak. The grocer will be able to claim they're giving customers more product, and you'll get great exposure. Are you in the fertilizer business? Find a weed-killer or garden tool company and package samples (or full product) with them. You can maintain your own brand or company identity—but customers love the value of convenience.

Co-branding

What is it? Co-branding is where your product or service mingles with that of a partner.

When should you use it? If the products are not only used together, but integrated as part of the same usage, co-branding makes sense.

When should you not use it? If one brand is much stronger, or the brands are unrelated, cobranding will weaken the brands.

How much should it cost per person reached? Co-branding expands the audience for each brand, so lower total cost per exposure.

Ben & Jerry's Coffee Heath Bar Crunch ice cream. SBC Yahoo DSL Internet service. DirecTV TiVo service. The Eddie Bauer Edition of the Ford Expedition sport utility vehicle. Co-branding is everywhere.

So how can you co-brand? You don't need to be nationally or internationally famous. Just find a known brand that's well thought of by your customers and would blend with your product or service. Your brand doesn't even need to be mixed with a corporate brand—a public institution may work as well, for example, "Firehouse #67 Blend Coffee," and "State House level service."

Pick wisely, and some of that rose scent will rub off on you.

Parting Thought: Awareness Isn't Sales

An old saying goes, "It is sometimes better to remain silent and be thought a fool than to open your mouth and be proven one."

If you seek to generate awareness, be sure you're prepared for success. If you attract a lot of attention and fail to deliver what you promised, you're actually in a worse position than if you'd gained no attention at all. Now you're known as the "don't go to them" guys... and a negative reputation is harder to change than no reputation at all.

What's more, awareness isn't a sale. You will probably need to make repeated contact with customers. Plan on additional steps after awareness— this is just the first part of marketing to a sale.

Those warnings issued, never fear—get your business ready, take your time planning who to make aware of your offering, and how to do it in a nonintrusive, helpful way, and then announce yourself to the world in good conscience and be ready to take the next step toward sales.

Chapter 5

Capture Contacts
Trade Business Cards

"Garbage In = Garbage Out"

—"The Impact of Computers on Accounting," 1964

IF YOU DON'T MAKE CONTACT WITH ANYONE, YOU CAN'T SELL ANYTHING. TO make a sale, you need to make contact with prospective purchasers. No contact, no sale. So before launching your awareness programs, whatever they may be—newspaper ads, a trade-show booth, an "e-mail blast"—think about how you can include mechanisms that will convert recipients into an actionable list of contactable prospective buyers.

Don't be shy. Your goal is to get your prospective customers' information. Get their names. Get their e-mail addresses, phone numbers, and fax numbers. Get their physical addresses. *Get all the details that you need to reach them again, and be sure they have your corresponding contact information so that they can find you at least as easily.*

Sound simple? It isn't. In this era of SPAM e-mail, identity theft, junk faxes, and information overload, few people with *real* purchasing power simply hand over their contact information. They're afraid of being deluged with sales solicitations, or worse. The people who are readily willing to give you their contact information probably aren't the ones with real power. So you can't just rely on luck or a great smile. You'll need to take a formal approach to collecting contacts, and use people's built-in psychology and needs to motivate them to *want* to give you their information.

This chapter will provide you with three guidelines for great contact capture. Follow the guidelines, and your prospective customers will not only stand in line to give you their contact information, they'll actually look forward to your call.

Following are the three guiding principles of contact capture:

- ► **Offer tools, not tchatchkes:** Offer the right incentive for capture.
- ► *Set up "the trade":* Invoke the force of reciprocity, and implement mechanisms for initial contact capture.
- ► **Recycle (recapture)/Do it again on the same dollar:** Understand the value of and techniques for additional information capture.

Obtaining prospective customers' contact information *is* critical to your business. If set up correctly, contact capture doesn't have to be a stressful, complex, or a high-effort activity. Still not convinced? Next time you meet someone, offer them your business card—and watch them return the favor by offering theirs. Congratulations, you just captured a contact.

Offer Tools, Not Tchatchkes

Rule number one of contact capture: *Offer your target contact something useful in exchange for their contact information.*

Rule number one of contact capture: Offer your target contact something useful in exchange for their contact information.

Bad marketers hear the word "offer" and miss the word "useful". They hand out tchatchkes. A tchatchke (pronounced "chotch-key") is the Americanized Yiddish word for "toy" or "trinket." Examples of tchatchke abuse range from simple to complex—from the balls, pens, and other "promotional items" handed out by vendors at trade shows in exchange for attendee business cards, to the $10 Starbucks gift cards Fidelity gave to each person who returned a postcard from a direct-mail campaign. It's not unusual for companies to spend thousands or tens of thousands of dollars on such giveaways.

But do tchatchke giveaways really produce valuable, lead-generating contacts? Why should someone with real purchasing power give you their contact information—allowing a way of disturbing them—in exchange for a *toy*?

Great entrepreneurial marketers know that trading contacts for toys is often (worse than) useless—that trading toys for contacts can actually add lots of useless contacts to your lists, masking the truly valuable contacts you need to reach. *What you give away makes a statement about how much or how little you value the contact information of the recipient. They'll respond in kind.*

So before spending on toys, think through your situation and goals. Be sure you understand the following:

▶ Why toys are useless for contact capture

▶ How to check to see if your situation is different

▶ What to use instead to capture contacts

Why Toys Are Useless

If toys are useless, why are they so commonly used in marketing? Bad marketers believe that trade-show attendees and promotional offer respondents are prequalified leads. These marketers reason that since someone went to the effort of attending a show or replying to a solicitation, that person is demonstrating interest in the marketer's business, and a toy is necessary to lure the attendee into providing contact information.

But this thinking is wrong. In fact, the most valuable contacts will be the ones most *reluctant* to share their contact information. The people who will happily part with their contact information and time in exchange for toys are motivated by the (low) value of the toy. They're exactly the audience you *don't* want.

The most valuable contacts will be the ones most reluctant to share their contact information.

Most toys don't even extend the awareness of your company—the exception being viral vehicles, as discussed in Chapters 3 and 4. A giveaway Frisbee isn't going to boost awareness of your company unless you're a Frisbee manufacturer and the Frisbee contains your company name, logo, web address, and a short benefit tagline indicating why your Frisbee is superior to any other. Still skeptical? Ask yourself how many companies or products you've pursued *solely* because you saw their name on a toy. (Not a product; viral applications of useful products are valid—but most giveaways are toys, not useful items.)

Promotional pens stay in pockets. Foam animals get left behind in office moves, or chewed up by pets. T-shirts are great if your prospects wear them at work—otherwise, they end up as moth food. All of these items cost you money, and none of them spread your message, help you obtain the right people's contact information, or generate lead flow.

How To Check

Still concerned that you'll be missing good prospects if you don't hand out toys? Test the theory during your next promotion to ascertain the motivational and awareness-generation power of your offers. Here's how.

First, you'll assess the unprompted contact-capture power of your offer. Create several hundred inexpensive, traditional giveaways that are unrelated to your product—for example, pens or foam hand exercisers. On each, print your company name, logo, and a dedicated phone number, fax number, or special e-mail address or web address that is not otherwise published but contains a brief product description and opportunity to submit contact information to learn more about your company.

Give away all of the toys at a "prequalified" trade show or other promotional event by including them as a bag insert. (Or, if your business is more local—say, a lawn care agency—drive around the neighborhood and leave these on people's doorsteps.) Do not demand contact information or a visit to your booth or business in exchange for the toy. Simply give the toys away. (In fact, to preserve the integrity of the experiment, you shouldn't be contacting or interacting with these folks by other means.)

Over the next four weeks, assess the number of contacts you obtain from the toy contact address (e.g., count the number of people who responded via the phone, fax, etc. information printed on the toy). Calculate the total cost per contact based on the cost of all toys given away, divided by the number of responses you receive. As an added bonus, calculate likely total sales to those contacts.

You'll soon see that toys in and of themselves don't generate cost-effective awareness. Simply publicly burning the dollars you spent would have gotten more attention.

Next, check the power of your offers to motivate the right behavior by the right people. Do your toys persuade prospective cash-bearing customers to call you?

Divide your target audience into three groups. If you're at a trade show, you can run each promotion for an hour, on a rotating basis. If you're doing your promotion via e-mail, give each third person a different offer. If you're a local business, at each house drop off one of three flyers which can be mailed in to claim the reward, or offer a phone number for people to call to get their reward.

Your three offers should be as follows:

▶ The first offer should be a traditional "toy" offer. Offer a T-shirt, pen, or gift of your choice—or set up a raffle (for example, offer a $3,000 television to one out of every thousand respondents).

▶ The second offer should be cash—actual dollar bills. Make the value comparable to the gift cost to your company. For example, if your pens in the first offer above cost $3 each, offer $3 in cash.

▶ The third offer should be information. Use information that's of career-furthering use to your prospect audience, and not easily available elsewhere. For example, you could offer a copy of an industry report, security audit, or other hard-to-obtain material created by a well-known analyst. Again, be sure the cost of the information is comparable to your other offers. For example, if the report cost you $3,000 for 1,000 copies, it's worth $3 each. This approach even applies to simple businesses, such as a lawn care service—your "report" could be as simple as "Brochure on the top lawn care tasks for each month of the year, to keep your lawn looking great."

Next, capture contacts. Trade the promotional items you created in offers one, two, and three for contact information of potential prospects. Ideally you won't just trade for your prospects' business cards. Instead, trade in exchange for their completing a survey. By using a survey instead of a simple contact card, you'll be able to collect additional qualifying information. For example, you could ask about their degree of experience with or interest in your product, amount of budget available to spend, and timeframe for evaluation or purchase.

Now, sort through the information you've captured. Assuming that your offer was worth less than $10, and that your product is worth substantially more than that, the highest volume of *contacts* will almost certainly be associated with the cash offer.

But the highest number of *actual potential leads*—contacts that turn into sales—will be associated with the information offer. This will be increasingly true as your product market is more highly priced, business-critical, and more complex.

So how do you get great contacts?

What To Offer Instead of Toys

As the prior experiments demonstrate, if you can offer something of *low cost to you and high value to your target prospects* (and only your target prospects), you stand a good chance of them trading something of similarly disparately perceived value in return—such as their contact information.

Toys *don't* fit the above definition. Their value and cost are comparable and easily assessed, and they offer the same utility—they're equally useful—to prospects and nonprospects alike.

Product-specific information, such as a brochure on your products, *doesn't* fit the above definition. It is worth more to you to persuade a prospect to read your brochure than it is for them to read it.

Information that validates decisions—that makes people sure they made the right choice in choosing you, or at least won't get fired for that decision—is valuable to them, even if it costs you little.

General industry information—career-applicable research—*fits* the above definition. If people's careers are made or lost on purchase and implementation of your product, the perceived value of the information you're giving them may dramatically exceed the actual cost to you of obtaining and providing that information. *Information that validates decisions—that makes people sure they made the right choice in choosing you, or at least won't get fired for that decision—is valuable to them, even if it costs you little.* So industry information becomes a very compelling offer, but only to the target segment, the right people.

As another example, consider the value to *you* (as a marketer) of a study showing the relative costs of different advertising, or a study showing the departments in target companies who are the most likely to spend money on your type of product in the coming year. Wouldn't you rather have that information from a vendor than a pen?

Alternatively, imagine yourself buying a car. Wouldn't you be willing to leave your contact information with (and buy from) the dealership who gave you a free copy of the *Consumer Reports* automobile buying guide, a local Better Business Bureau report on local dealer honesty, or a chart of the automobile's repair record and resale value over time (all stamped with the dealer's phone number and name, of course)? Contrast your willingness to trade a business card for that information with your (un)willingness to trade a business card to a dealer in exchange for some fuzzy dice, or a nice pen.

So don't rely on toys. Offer your customers generally applicable information, such as reports that can:

- help them compare and learn about many products (not just yours) in an unbiased manner,
- make the return-on-investment case for your product,
- help them understand their or your industry,
- help them understand what other products and services to deploy to fully solve their problem (a "solution" or "ecosystem" view of their problem) and where your offering fits, and

▶ help them look good within their company while exerting less effort to do so.

In sum—*skip the pen; offer paper(s).*

Summary: Why offer tools, not toys? Because tools attract the right type of potential contact.

▶ Toys attract people looking for free things, not people looking to pay you for things.

▶ You can check this by doing two offers and seeing which yields more actual paid business.

▶ Information is cheap to produce and attracts the right type of customer. Use it.

Set Up "The Trade"

Large companies routinely pay tens of thousands of dollars for market research, and hundreds of thousands of dollars to set up customer focus groups. Obviously, information has value.

But not all information has equal value, or equal costs. An 8.5" × 11" sheet of paper describing your product serves *you* as much as or more than it serves your customer. So a prospective customer might be skeptical if asked to *pay* for that datasheet.

In contrast, an industry report serves the prospective *customers'* needs. The report helps them do their job better, improving their value to their employer, and thus their compensation. So the customer might be gratified to learn that they can "pay" for that report merely by providing their contact information for future sales follow-up.

Good entrepreneurial marketers understand how to balance the cost of information assembly, the value of information, and the need for contact capture. They understand:

▶ Why to force a trade,

▶ When to trade and when to give information away, and

▶ How to set up the trade.

Good entrepreneurial marketers understand how to balance the cost of information assembly, the value of information, and the need for contact capture.

Why Force A Trade?

Begging isn't as effective as trading. There is a difference in the types of prospects you will obtain, and the behavior you'll obtain from those prospects, when you make an *explicit* trade for their contact information instead of freely and indiscriminately handing out your information and *then* asking (begging) for their contact data.

This is not to say that information should never be made freely available to your potential customer base; rather, it is a warning that you should be aware of what value is associated with which information, and make the trade explicit, if subtle. You'd think poorly of a merchant who priced tin at $300 per ounce but gave away gold for free—so make sure you're not doing the same with your information assets.

You'd think poorly of a merchant who priced tin at $300 per ounce but gave away gold for free—so make sure you're not doing the same with your information assets.

Forcing a trade entails making an *explicit* request for your prospective customers' contact information before providing something in return. Trading is necessary for contact capture because reciprocity—the principle that states that all humans will innately respond to being given something by giving in return—will fail in a high-volume, impersonal environment. In other words, handing someone a business card in a one-on-one situation will almost always result in their handing you their card. But putting out a pile of business cards on a display table will rarely result in other folks leaving theirs in exchange.

Consider: In a personal one-on-one exchange, reciprocity works. You may be willing to give a salesperson your business card after they give you a report because you've established a degree of personal relationship. They've given you something, you feel obligated to return the favor—but if you obtain the report from a company web site, you'll ignore a message asking for your e-mail address *after* you downloaded it. The personal connection wasn't made, and reciprocity isn't in effect. Countless authors of "shareware" software (software that is free to download, but asks the user to donate a nominal fee to the developer after use) can testify to the small percentages of users who actually "pay up." So ask for payment (contact information) up front.

Remember, your most desirable prospects are the ones with budget and interest in your product. Since they are actively interested in the valuable information you have, they should be willing to make a trade. You can set the "price" of the trade to match their desire, in terms of how much information you require and how much you'll use it to contact them later—but serious prospects should "ante up." As an entrepreneur, your budget for contact capture and subsequent lead parsing is small: Wouldn't you rather have five good leads (and miss two) than risk having no measured leads at all (but many distributed whitepapers)?

So why force a trade? The answer is simple: In order to get better prospects.

When To Trade, When To Give It Away

Some information should be freely distributed. Some shouldn't. You may be giving too much away already.

Consider: If you asked each prospective customer for $20 before sending them a catalog, you might end up with many fewer prospects for your goods—or, you might end up with an extra revenue stream, depending on the content of your catalog. Seem unlikely? Magazines charge subscriptions—and several high-end retailers charge for catalogs. The delicate balance is knowing when to trade what information. The two factors to weigh when assessing whether information is worth forcing a trade are *stage in purchase cycle* and *inherent information value.*

Stage in the purchase cycle is the more easily assessed aspect of information trade. As discussed in Chapter 1, contact capture occurs *after* awareness generation. You should *trade* information *after* awareness consideration, when your prospect has been made aware of your product, and has entered the consideration stage of the purchasing process. Don't attempt to trade before the consideration phase; your prospect needs to be sufficiently aware of the issues and your product to know what questions to ask.

In other words, *give away* enough information to generate awareness—to get people to know your name and become interested in what you could do for them. Then *trade* more specific information for their contact information.

Inherent information value is more difficult to assess, but is defined by the focus of the information you're offering: internal or external.

Information designed to promote awareness, used to make the prospective customer aware of your company, is *inwardly* focused and designed to be as freely and widely proliferated as possible. Basics about what your company and product do, what the fundamental benefits are, and how to obtain more information are examples of such *inwardly* focused information. Getting your customer to read this information has more value to you than to your customer. This is information your company generates. Product specifications and *your* contact information should not only be free, you actually pay to push that information out as advertising.

Conversely, *externally* focused information is information that is transportable across companies instead of specific to your company, and allows prospective customers insight on the larger industry. This information has higher utility to your customers than to you. This is information typically generated by an independent third party. It is not information you can cre-

Information designed to promote awareness, used to make the prospective customer aware of your company, is inwardly focused and designed to be as freely and widely proliferated as possible.

ate from within your company in a manner that will be perceived as unbiased and thus valuable to customers. Surveys about the industry, comparisons between your offering and others, and information about *their* environment is externally focused information, and externally focused information makes a valuable trade good.

So if your information serves no other purpose than to inform people about your product, it should be free. It sells your product. Conversely, if your information helps people do their job (and happens to involve your product), it's a trade good. You trade it for their contact information.

Also, your information should only have value to prospective customers, and no others—so through the very act of information distribution, an initial lead filtering and screening process will occur. Only prospective customers will be *willing* to trade their information for yours; well-chosen information is valueless to nonprospects.

Still have doubts about what parts of your information is of value and what isn't? Survey your customers. Ask them for feedback on which studies, articles, and reports (internal or external) helped them make their purchasing decision. Then go acquire some.

How To Set Up The Trade

If you want something from your customer in exchange for what you're giving them, be sure they understand that there will be a trade, and that the trade will be to their benefit.

Trades of information for contacts are and should be explicit. If you want something from your customer in exchange for what you're giving them, be sure they understand that there will be a trade, and that the trade will be to their benefit.

For example, salespeople say "Just give me your business card and I'll send you that information you wanted." Web sites ask for your contact information and preferences before allowing you to see whitepapers, read news articles, or download evaluation copies of software. Customer support phone numbers ask for your information "to better assist you." You're asking for something of value from your prospective customer; be sure your customer understands that they're getting something of value in return.

There are three steps to setting up your trade for contact information: *obtaining goods to trade, making your prospective customers aware of your product and tradable goods,* and *executing the trade.*

Obtaining goods to trade is a matter of obtaining information of high value to your prospects, but low per-prospect cost to you, as described in the prior section. You can purchase a redistributable magazine or industry report, create your own report by surveying your customer base or doing a technical study, or provide a useful ancillary tool or service. Common examples of these goods are reprints of consumer digest reports or multi-product competitive reviews, whitepapers, reprints of technical journal articles, recorded video or PowerPoint presentations of conference sessions on industry or technical subjects (made available online or on DVD), software-based "sizing guides," "capacity planners," or "usage analysis tools," or even constrained free access to complementary industry data stores, sponsored by your company. (For example, in exchange for contact information, a mutual fund company sponsored 30-day free access to online mutual-fund rating and research service Morningstar Premium.) Even such basic services as lawn care and dry-cleaning can provide consumer-oriented "tip sheets" and helpful research.

Once you have valuable trade goods, you must *make consumers aware of your product and valuable information*. When engaging in the product awareness activities described in the prior chapter, include mention of your valuable information—it's an effective lure, or "call to action." For example, your materials might say, "Come find out more about YourCo today by visiting our web site at www.yourco.com/offer_2 or stop by our booth #116 at the upcoming trade show YourWorld, and *receive a complimentary copy of the latest Forrester research report on YourIndustry.*" Ideally, you can tempt prospects by actually giving them a taste of the information—perhaps citing a particularly compelling line or two from the research report, or other content. For example, consider *Sports Illustrated* magazine. Postcards advertising the *Sports Illustrated* swimsuit edition are aggressively distributed, many featuring a sample photo from the magazine. The potential subscribers are given a taste of what to expect. But once aware of the magazine, when contacts enter the consideration phase of purchasing, they are asked to submit contact information in trade for more "valuable" information, such as additional samples or discounted subscription rate information.

So *tempt* prospective customers with a taste of your information. Then *trade* them the rest, along with some of your product information, in exchange for their contact information.

Finally, you must *execute the trade*. When customers call, fax, visit your trade show booth or web site, or otherwise respond to your offer to trade, you must capture their contact information and deliver the promised reward.

When capturing information, be aware of the value you're providing, and set the "price" of your goods accordingly. A prospective customer will probably be willing to enter their e-mail address on a web site in exchange for being e-mailed a copy of a research report or whitepaper—especially if

Tempt prospective customers with a taste of your information. Then trade them the rest, along with some of your product information, in exchange for their contact information.

the web site promises that the prospect will only receive one follow-up e-mail or can opt-out of marketing at any time. The same prospective customer may not be willing to complete a 12-page survey of their buying habits, provide their date of birth and mother's maiden name, or submit to a blood test to obtain the same information. Although the temptation is to attempt to extract the maximum qualification information possible from the prospect—their budget, purchase timeframe, credit card number—the prospect's perception of the value you're demanding must be commensurate with the value they perceive you're delivering.

The most ingenious mechanisms are those that combine the contact capture with the delivery of value, in a nonintrusive manner. The simplest and most transparent example is requesting an e-mail alias so that a whitepaper can be sent. No contact provided equals no value delivered. Similar existing examples include asking for a Social Security number and address to provide the prospect with a free credit report (mortgage industry), or asking for specific details of equipment the prospect owns, so that a custom report on power consumption can be calculated (computer hardware industry). In all cases, the contact capturing company's capture mechanism is self-qualifying; if prospective customers want value out of the system, they have to put value in.

Summary: What's "the trade"? Offering relevant information as a *trade* for contact information, instead of simply giving it away, yields higher-quality leads.

- ▶ Force a trade instead of giving information away because it will improve your lead quality: Only truly interested people who value your targeted information will provide contact information.
- ▶ Trade information that is valuable to your customers. Give away information that's valuable to you (i.e., that you need them to have).
- ▶ Create information that is valuable to your customer by using existing data (reprints) or aggregating survey information provided by your own customers, then deliver it to them using the contact information they provide.

Recycle (Recapture): Do It Again on the Same Dollar

When you dial 411—directory assistance—on a telephone, you expect to pay a significant fee to acquire the contact information—the telephone number or address—that you are seeking.

As a one-time cost, you probably consider the 411 fee quite reasonable, in part because you then record the phone number for later use. The total cost of that call to directory assistance is spread out, amortized over the number of times you use the phone number you obtained, and so the cost per call of that 411 fee becomes insignificant.

This basic logic seems to escape many bad salespeople and marketers, who persist in repeatedly leasing one-time-use mail or telephone contact lists—doing the equivalent of dialing directory assistance before every call, and never recording the phone number for later use.

Good entrepreneurial managers understand how to leverage their initial investments in awareness and contact capture for subsequent re-use—capturing contacts by not letting them go. They understand the following aspects of the capture:

► Capture versus recapture

► Relative costs

► Setting up recapture

Capture versus Recapture

The difference in contact value between an initially captured contact and a subsequently recaptured contact is the level of specific commitment to your company exhibited by the prospective customer whose contact information is involved. *If you get them once, you can invite them back. If they come back, they're interested in you and likely to be an easier sale.*

This process of contact recapture and qualification can also be thought of as "lead maturation"—the process by which a prospective customer is exposed to successively more education and guided through the purchase process.

Consider these different levels of capture and recapture:

► If you purchase a one-time mailing list from a magazine, you've obtained a one-use list of contacts. But these contacts have no commitment to you or your product. They may not even have any awareness of you and your product.

► If you contact the members of the list, and lure some back to your web site, where they trade their e-mail address to you in exchange for a whitepaper, you've engaged in first-level recapture: This subset is now more aware and committed to you. You also now own their e-mail addresses as an asset—and as long as they don't opt-out of your mar-

Good entrepreneurial managers understand how to leverage their initial investments in awareness and contact capture for subsequent re-use—capturing contacts by not letting them go.

keting, you can re-use (re-contact) that asset several times, reducing your initial effective one-time list cost.

▶ If you then re-contact the list members who provided their e-mail addresses, and lure them back to complete a more comprehensive set of contact questions in exchange for a larger-value item (for example, invitation to a seminar, a trial of your product, or other more company-specific event or offer), you've engaged in second-level or greater recapture: The bonds being forged between your company and the potential prospects are increasingly strengthened.

Every marketing program you do should be designed to recapture. Always strive to keep them coming back for more.

Relative Costs

Contact recapture will change the relative cost of any external list rental, so it's critical to factor in the effects to optimize your marketing spending.

Contact recapture will change the relative cost of any external list rental, so it's critical to factor in the effects to optimize your marketing spending.

Financially, a rental list that may initially appear less expensive on a cost-per-contact basis may turn out to be quite expensive if it offers minimal recapture. If your list costs $15,000 for 1,000 names, but offers a 50 percent recapture rate, you'll get at least 1,500 contact opportunities (initial 1,000 + 50 percent of the initial 1,000 recaptured), lowering the effective cost per contact by more than 30 percent, to $10 per contact. Conversely, if you had purchased a different list for only $12,000 that had a 10 percent recapture rate, you'd only obtain 1,100 contact opportunities, providing you with an effectively 10 percent higher cost of approximately $11 per contact—and this example assumes only a one-time, first-stage recapture.

Factoring recapture into list purchase makes strategic sense as well as financial sense—the recapture rate should be directly related to the quality of the contacts as leads, unless you artificially inflate recapture by offering "toys," as previously discussed. If you've purchased a list of people who are *appropriate* prospects for your product, a high percentage will likely be interested in your information offer, and respond. Conversely, if your purchased list was *poorly* chosen, your recapture rate will reflect the disinterest in your services, unless your offer is attractive to more than your prospect set (e.g., the offer is cash, not targeted information), at which point your response and recapture rate will be artificially distorted. Artificial negative distortion can also occur, if you're asking for too high a "price" for your offering. A high response rate but low actual contact recapture—lots of clicks to your response page but no registrations—may indicate that you're

94

asking for too much contact information, or that your initial communication of your offer was misleading.

Of course, a good recapture program will involve several rounds of recapture. Before completing your calculations, it's important to understand the repeat recapture rate—how many times customers must be contacted before buying or "opting out." For example, if you see 10 percent of your customers opting out after each round of marketing communication, you have only six or seven rounds until you've lost half of your original recaptured list. If, by analyzing your existing customers, you understand that most buy after seven rounds of communication, you'll need to plan your initial list purchases to account for the subsequent 50 percent drop-off in a subsequent likely purchasing population.

A good recapture program will involve several rounds of recapture.

Setting Up Recapture

So how do you set up recapture? There are three aspects to consider; *frequency*, *capture depth*, and *publicity*.

Frequency addresses the speed with which you can effectively use marketing communications to deepen the relationship between your prospective customer and your company. For example, if your customers don't mind being contacted weekly, you might ask for successively greater information from them through weekly calls or e-mails, where the first starts with a "give us your e-mail address and we'll send you a whitepaper" level of trade, and subsequent contacts quickly move to more substantive information trades. If your customers prefer a lower but more significant level of contact, recapture may take fewer, longer, higher-touch meetings—for example, phone surveys and in-person collection of business cards and other information. The higher the frequency, the more automated recapture infrastructure can be put in place, and the more people you can reach at lower cost.

Capture depth addresses the amount of contact information requested from prospects, both per interaction and in total. Asking for a contact's first name (only) is low depth. Asking for their e-mail address, phone number, and physical address is of higher depth. Asking for their budget, expected purchasing timeframe, and other demographics is of even greater depth. The deeper the information you need, the harder it is to get, the longer it will take to get, and the more it will cost to get.

Publicity addresses the degree to which you publicize your recapture opportunities. Minimal publicity would be a linear model: You send an e-mail, with a link back to an otherwise unlinked (hidden) web page/short registration form—for example, you ask for their e-mail address to send them a whitepaper. The registrants are sent a second e-mail en masse, with a link back to a second, deeper recapture opportunity (such as a webinar or seminar registration, with additional questions). There's a direct cause and effect, and it's easy to track the progress of a group. At the other end of the spectrum, maximal publicity would feature all registration pages concurrently available and linked openly from your web site. Customers would self-select into different offers, and all communications from the company would cross-link to other contact-capture opportunities. Behind the scenes, a database would asynchronously fill in the various information fields captured by various offers—and a contact would be declared a "qualified lead" once a certain number of fields had passed their thresholds.

To set up recapture, first understand the sum total of information that you'll need to "qualify" a prospect (Budget? Interest level?) and the minimal information that you'd need to re-contact them (E-mail address? Phone?). Phrase this as a giant questionnaire. Then, based on your understanding of their preferred frequency, and your ability to parse their responses synchronously or asynchronously, proceed to split up the questionnaire into as many subquestionnaires as needed, each with an associated item traded to the prospect responding, and each featured in one or more communications vehicles (possibly feeding each other, with respondents from one being redirected to the "next step" offer. Gave us your name? Come register for the webinar and give us your address.).

Make sure the first recapture step captures the minimal contact information, then launch the first communication setting the system in motion, and let your contact capture machine do its work.

Summary: Why recapture? Recapture lowers total cost of contact acquisition, while simultaneously filtering and educating for better lead quality.

▶ Recapture refers to the process of collecting information for subsequent marketing contact use from people who have responded to an offer sent to a third-party rented list.

▶ Recapture makes sense because it effectively lowers your cost of contact: If you can reach the same person twice without any additional rental fees, your cost is effectively halved.

▶ Recapture can be a linear or parallel process, ask for lots of information at each contact or little, and can be frequent or occasional—the exact choices depend on your offering and target audience's receptiveness.

Parting Thought: Don't Interrupt Their Dinner

No one likes having their dinner interrupted by people who want money. More generally, in this era of radically increased privacy concerns and sensitivity, no one likes sharing their personal information ... and any practice that even hints at abuse of the trust that contact-givers have placed in you will immediately have severe negative repercussions.

It is critical that you follow good privacy practices to successfully capture contacts. Failure to do so will at best end their marketing efforts; at worst, it will result in federal legal troubles. Before engaging in any marketing, be sure to understand the CAN-SPAM legislation on e-mail as well as the associated legislation on junk faxes, telemarketing, and junk mail. (A hint: They all basically say, "don't bother people who haven't signed up to get information from you; be honest about who you are and how to reach you when you reach them; and provide a way for them to tell you to stop contacting them.")

So before engaging in contact capture and recapture practices, do three things:

> ▶ **Establish a "privacy policy"**: This policy explains in clear language what you will and won't do with the contact information you've captured.

> ▶ **Establish an "opt out" mechanism**: This means including your physical business address, phone number, and process for opting out in *all* communications you send.

> ▶ **Honor that policy and process**: Don't share contact information with other businesses, don't delay in removing people from your contact list, and examine your marketing: A subtle, effective marketer won't be generating lots of opt-out requests, that's a sign you're not communicating useful information to the right people in a way they'll accept.

In short, treat your customers at least as well as you'd like to be treated. Don't annoy them, don't waste their time, don't overexpose them to your marketing (or worse, someone else's) —and don't ever call them at dinnertime.

No one likes sharing their personal information ... and any practice that even hints at abuse of the trust that contact-givers have placed in you will immediately have severe negative repercussions.

Chapter 6

Qualify Leads ... and Sell
Ask Them to Pay for Lunch

"There's a world of difference between involvement and commitment. At a ham and egg meal, for example, the chicken is involved, but the pig is committed."

—Common folk saying

"There is no such thing as a free lunch."

—Phrase popularized by Milton Friedman, Economist, in his 1975 book by the same name

"Show me the money, Jerry! Show me the money! Show me the money!"

—Tom Cruise and Cuba Gooding Jr., in the movie *Jerry McGuire*

IF NONE OF YOUR CONTACTS WILL BUY FROM YOU, IT DOESN'T MATTER HOW many contacts you have. On payday, it is more important to have made one sale than to have talked to 1,000 contacts. Contacts are not yet leads. *Leads* turn into sales, but *contacts* may just go to lunch on your tab and waste your time. *If you pick the wrong contacts at the beginning of the quarter, they won't turn into sales at the end of the quarter.*

Making your marketing programs count—turning them into sales—means not only generating contacts, but also generating *qualified leads*. Good marketing programs separate *valuable* prospective customers from the remainder of your acquired contacts.

Do you know who among your contacts has direct purchasing authority, who makes the decision to buy (even if they're not the person signing the check to you), and who has other degrees of influence on purchasing? Do you know who has available budget, and how much they have to spend? Do you know who has a deadline to make a decision, and who is still in the early stages of research about various solutions? *Keeping your business alive means using your marketing to find out who* needs *to buy now, who is trying to convince the check writer to buy, who is just doing research, and who is just wasting your time.*

This chapter will show you how to build the right elements into your marketing programs to ensure you produce a high-quality set of leads. You *can* improve quality *without* significant additional expense by properly preplanning and integrating filters and tests into the contact-gathering process, and using the social dynamics of nonfinancial motivators and commitment to separate good *intentions* from good *leads*.

By the end of the chapter, you will know how to successfully:

▶ **Establish commitment instead of participation:** Define a qualified lead.

▶ **Assess interest and means and cause:** Check a contact's qualifications as a lead.

▶ **Watch the hands, not the mouth:** Use behavioral analysis to verify that contact's qualifications.

Your selling time is worth money to your business. It can make you money—but it always *costs* you money. Selling time is time you're not doing other things. So you need to make more money per hour than you're missing making by doing those other things. Don't waste your sales time looking for the needle—the one good lead—in a haystack of contacts. Set up a system to prequalify leads, to spin your straw into gold, so that you can spend your sales time closing business deals and collecting checks instead of scrabbling in the pile for leads.

Making your marketing programs count—turning them into sales—means not only generating contacts, but also generating qualified leads.

Establish Commitment Instead of Participation

An effective, albeit aggressive, method of lead qualification is to ask your prospective customer to "put their money where their mouth is." Ask them for commitment, typically via an up-front investment of some type, *before* starting the process of selling them the actual product or service.

Why require an investment from your customer prior to the actual sale? Because investment moves people from *involvement* to *commitment*. Think about the last time you bought an automobile—were you asked to put down a (completely) refundable deposit to "hold" the vehicle? Did you consider other vehicles as seriously after your commitment to the one with the deposit? Your mental commitment followed your cash.

Commitment reflects a level of mental, financial, or legal involvement where the prospective purchaser faces a higher level of hardship and stress if they *don't* proceed to purchase—where, to use the chicken and pig illustration, the expenditure to that point appears so great (you've killed the pig) that *failure* to complete the process (not serving breakfast) would appear to be a greater loss than would be completing it.

Commitment reflects a level of mental, financial, or legal involvement where the prospective purchaser faces a higher level of hardship and stress if they don't proceed to purchase.

So why do entrepreneurial marketers care about getting commitment? The answer is that obtaining *commitment* from a prospective customer during the marketing process dramatically increases the probability of your completing a *sale*. If commitment can be obtained in a scaleable, inexpensive manner, you make money. You win.

Correspondingly, good entrepreneurial managers understand:

▶ What commitment is,

▶ Why commitment works, and

▶ How to obtain commitment.
  ### What Commitment Is

Commitment reflects the mental shift created when your marketing persuades a prospective customer to take a seemingly irreversible step toward a sale. In other words, if a customer agrees to your request to jump into a mud puddle with a white shirt on, they're showing commitment to obtaining some sort of laundry services later—ideally *your* services.

Commitment can take the form of a verbal agreement, written agreement, set of actions, or exchange of goods, services, or cash. The *form* of commitment is less important than the *result*.

Moreover, the challenges created by "backing out" don't need to be financial. The threat of social embarrassment, career-threatening company losses, and loss of time and effort also generate commitment.

For example, if your prospect promised their boss something would be completed, it may be more embarrassing for *them* to admit their purchasing mistake than for *you* to take the blame. If they've spent 40 hours meeting with you, it may be simpler to purchase your offering instead of repeating the 40 hours with another vendor.

In short, *if you can create a situation where the prospective customer finds it easier to move forward with you than to back out, you have commitment.*

Why Commitment Works

Commitment works because it uses people's brains against them. They are selling *themselves* on your offering—you're just helping. The fact is that people are socially and biologically conditioned to act in logical, consistent ways. They won't commit themselves to a course of action if they don't believe they are planning to follow that course of action. For example, you wouldn't jump into that mud puddle if you didn't believe laundry was in your future.

What this logical approach results in is that even when the commitment itself carries no apparent penalty, there's an inherent psychological cost to breaking the commitment. As Robert Cialdini points out, this behavior is inescapable. Everyone's brain works this way—it's a reflex.

Customers won't commit themselves to a course of action if they don't believe they are planning to follow that course of action.

But the result of this biological conditioning is that if you commit to an action, you're likely to complete this action, even if there's no penalty for not completing it. For example, if you put a 100 percent refundable, no questions asked, 24-hour deposit down on a car, you won't go back and reclaim your deposit and buy a different car. You can't renege without violating the original premise under which you put down the deposit.

By reclaiming the deposit, you'd be saying that either you are inconsistent (you were serious enough to put down a deposit and hold the car, but could reverse that seriousness in 24 hours), you are irrational (you put down the deposit because you didn't want to buy the car), or you always intended to reclaim the deposit and were not honest with the salesperson (you're not a "good" person). But your brain will resist this behavior. It will work against you, in favor of maintaining your commitment. So you'll buy the car.

In short, people are biologically set up in such a way that they don't like to think (or *can't* act in ways that make them think) that they made a "dumb" decision. So if you can get them to choose you, they're hooked. Marketing, assisted by biology, wins out over logic.

Obtaining Commitment

The most aggressive form of commitment is a sale. Once a product is "sold"—a contract signed, the product delivered, an invoice sent—the repercussions of a customer not paying can be severe. Yet you don't need to go as far as a sale to obtain commitment. Consider the other levels of commitment, as follows.

- ▶ **Time:** The more time someone has spent with you, the more reluctant they are to consider that time "wasted" by disposing of the relationship with you. So calculate the up-front odds of making a sale, and the value of that sale, and spend time accordingly. For example, if a sale is worth $1,000, and there's a 50-50 chance the sale will occur, the situation is worth $500 to you ($1,000 × 50%). At $50 per hour, it's worth 10 hours of your time. So take them out for coffee, present to them, call, send e-mail, and attempt to sell them… for 10 hours.

- ▶ **Information:** The more information your contact provides you—about their situation, their available budget, their decision process, their concerns—the more committed they are to you. But take your time obtaining that information—you wouldn't ask someone to marry you on the first date, so don't ask them their purchase intentions on the first call. Ask about their needs, their job, their concerns—then slowly move into discussing their available budget, decision-making power, authority, and the deeper issues.

- ▶ **Publicity:** Referrals, case studies, internal presentations to executives—the more public the commitment by your contact to your business, the stronger that commitment. It's like introducing your boyfriend or girlfriend to your parents—once your contact announces they're working with you, and introduces you to others, they're committed to you to a greater degree.

- ▶ **Cash or financial obligation:** Payment is hugely effective at generating commitment. Whether you get something as small as a "payment for a trial," or as large as a "down payment on the purchase," your prospective customer will be reluctant to ask for their money back, much less end the purchase process.

- ▶ **Legal obligation:** Contracts are almost as good as up-front cash—and sometimes better, in that contracts may stipulate payment in the event that the would-be purchaser changes their mind.

Again, commitment can be as simple as a handshake—just get your prospective customer to say those two magic words, "I agree" (to a meeting, payment, package you send them, *anything*) and they're yours.

Summary: Go beyond simply making contact—get commitment from your prospective customers.

▶ Commitment is a shift in your prospects' state of mind, wherein they invest in you.

▶ Commitment makes prospects more likely to buy from you.

▶ Commitment can take the form of a prospect investing time, information, publicity, legal obligations or cash in you.

Assess Interest and Means and Cause

There are varying levels of commitment. At its core, lead qualification is about answering a basic question: What's a prospective customer's proximity to purchase? How *likely* is a given prospective customer to buy, and how *much* will they buy? How "close" are they to buying?

The simplest way to answer that question is to ask the prospective customer. Unfortunately, prospective customers have grown wary of giving direct answers to those questions. They've been conditioned to expect that if they indicate readiness they'll be pushed to buy, and if they indicate lack of readiness they'll either be pushed for an explanation of barriers or they'll be ignored. Want to experience how this conditioning happens? Go to any large commission-based retail store. When a salesperson asks, "May I help you?" say no. You'll either be ignored, or immediately questioned about your barriers to buying. Either way, the experience is likely to raise your resistance to questioning in the future.

Furthermore, even if prospective customers *want* to give you a straightforward, honest answer, sometimes they can't. They may lack authority to make final purchasing decisions, or may lack knowledge about their company's larger plans—for all they know, their division may be about to be sold, and cancel all planned purchases, for example.

Yet successful entrepreneurial lead qualification *depends* on you being able to quickly, efficiently, "scaleably" extract a true answer to the purchasing proximity issue—and the simplest method to obtain this answer is still via a carefully designed set of filtering questions and responses.

How "close" is the customer to buying? The simplest way to answer that question is to ask.

103

Specifically, there are three aspects of your prospective customers you need to understand to begin to qualify them as leads. You need to know if they:

► Have interest.

► Have means.

► Have cause.

Have Interest

It might seem heretical to suggest that you have contacts who aren't interested in buying your product but who are in your prospect list or database. But every business has these contacts. There's a two-step process to separating out those contacts who are truly interested in purchasing from those who aren't: removal of those who *know* they're uninterested, and segregation for further processing of those who *think* they're interested but aren't yet at a purchasing level.

Your first task in lead-qualification questioning is to separate out the expressly uninterested contacts. Whether these folks are contacts who were once interested and now aren't, or are folks who were convinced to submit their name by a compelling offer but never had interest in your product, random names uploaded by sales from their Rolodex at a former job, or analysts interested in learning more about your company from a business perspective, they're *all* worse than worthless contacts.

Start separating wheat from chaff by asking first-stage separation questions. These could be included as response options on the direct-mail forms, web pages, or telemarketing scripts used to do initial contact capture or subsequent contact recapture—or the questions could be periodically sent as a separate survey to contacts.

Direct questions are fair—questions such as:

► How interested are you right now in our products/company, on a 1-to-5 scale?

► Has your interest level changed in the last three months? (On a scale of 1 to 5, 1 being a big decrease, 5 being a big increase)
  • If a decrease, why? (open response or set of options)
  • If an increase, why? (open response or set of options)

► How would you describe your interest?
  • thinking of purchasing (this quarter) (this year).
  • I'm just researching.

- I'm no longer interested, please delete my contact information. (May we contact you one last time to understand why?)

Most uninterested contacts will be honest in their responses—there's little incentive for them to waste their time with your sales team if they aren't purchasers. But you can segment your list and continue to push zero-cost awareness materials like e-mailed whitepapers to the "researching" contacts, while not spending *any* sales time with these contacts.

Your second task in lead-qualification questioning is to separate out the contacts who *believe* they're interested, but whose definition of "interested" doesn't qualify them as purchasers. There's a difference between prospects who think the product is "really cool" and those who are asking about the product's technical specifications. For the purposes of lead qualification, you want to spend your selling time only with contacts who are well educated about the product.

Separation in this stage involves both *explicit* questions and answers, and *implicit* answers—information gleaned from analysis of actual behavior. Actions sometimes speak louder than words.

On an *explicit* basis, you can ask questions such as the following:

▶ How would you rate your current knowledge of the product? (1 to 5)

▶ How would you rate your current knowledge of this technology? (1 to 5)

▶ How would you rate your current level of industry experience? (1 to 5)

▶ Have you used this type of product before? (Yes/No)

▶ Have you compared this product to other alternative solutions? (Yes/No)

▶ Have you engaged in any of the following? (Checkbox, and if web-based, questions may be cross-linked as appropriate—e.g., whitepaper question to whitepaper)
  - Visited company trade-show booth
  - Read whitepaper on product
  - Watched webinar on product
  - Attended seminar on product
  - Have taken trial of product

On an *implicit* basis, the question data should already be resident in your tracking spreadsheet—e.g., you should be keeping track of which offers are sent to which contacts and weighting the value of the leads based on actions accordingly. More detail on this follows in the third section of this chapter.

There's a difference between prospects who think the product is "really cool" and those who are asking about the product's technical specifications.

105

Having Means

Genuine interest in your product is a great first step toward being a qualified lead, but of course a good lead will also be able to buy your product. *Means* refers to having the necessary budget and the authority to spend it.

Like interest, means must be determined through *direct and explicit*, *indirect and explicit*, and *inferred* methods—because prospects may not realize when they do or don't have means to purchase (Have you checked your credit rating lately? Do you know how qualified a purchaser you are?), *and* may not want to subject themselves to increased sales attention. Don't understand that last comment? Put on a nice suit, Rolex watch, and carry a platinum American Express credit card and visit a commission-based car dealership. You won't be able to pry yourself away from the salespeople with a crowbar.

Furthermore, having both budget and spending authority is an increasingly rare combination as the product purchase price increases. Consider: In large companies, a department may have the necessary budget in total, but it may be earmarked for other projects. Purchases over a certain size may need CFO approval. Purchases may need to be routed through a purchasing department, which by default may demand the lowest-priced generic version of a product. In individual purchaser cases, a person's ability to buy from you may also suddenly shift, due to situation changes—job loss, for example.

So it's critical to determine early in the lead process whether a contact can buy from you, or whether they're associated with a purchaser but are not themselves a decision-maker. Then weight your leads accordingly, as the leads were weighted for "interest."

Direct and explicit questions are of less use in determining means, but can be used. Ask questions such as the following:

▶ What is your budget?

▶ Can you specify vendors, or are all contracts placed through the purchasing department? (Or, as an individual, who writes the checks/pays the bills in your household?)

▶ What is your maximum signing authority?/What is the most you'd pay for this?

Note that many prospects consider these questions intrusive, and may not be disposed to answer them. Indirect and explicit questions may be perceived as less intrusive, and so may be more successful in determining means. Ask questions such as the following:

Genuine interest in your product is a great first step toward being a qualified lead, but of course a good lead will also be able to buy your product.

- ▶ Have you purchased and implemented comparable-scale products over the past year? Which ones? (This can also allow a discussion of concerns in implementation, and value-added services you can provide.)

- ▶ How long has it taken paperwork to get through?/How long has it taken you to make your final decision? Could you describe the process? (This can be explained as a way of insuring that there's no delay in their order. Offer to trade information—describe how their order would be processed on your side, and how quickly.)

- ▶ Is there anything we should be aware of about your decision and purchase process as we try to best serve you? Anything unique to your company, or anything that has snagged other vendors?

Of course, the least intrusive approach is one that doesn't have to involve direct interaction at all—where this data may be obtained via third-party research, rather than direct questioning—such as the following:

- ▶ What is your/your company's size, number of employees, and credit record? (This also helps establish potential overall sale size.)

- ▶ What have been the major purchases you have made from other vendors? How many other vendors are suppliers? (An approximation of this data is available through a simple Internet search of press releases of major deals, or customer success stories by vendors.)

- ▶ Have you purchased from us before? What was the experience? What was the purchase process and organization?

Having Cause

Last but not least in your series of qualification questions are those about *cause*. Cause is a measure of time and flexibility. If your prospective customer has significant, business-critical cause to purchase, he'll purchase more quickly and is less likely to be sensitive to price or competitive issues. After all, if you had a deadline to implement a lead-generation program or be fired, you'd be less price-sensitive and more open to any vendor who could assist you.

Questions to determine cause are usually deadline- or project-focused. Explicit but relatively indirect questions work well, such as the following:

- ▶ Is there any time-sensitivity to this purchase?

- ▶ Is this product for a specific project, or just for experimentation? What is the project? (What are its deadlines, which group is funding it, how important is it to the organization?)

107

- ▶ Will you need this product delivery expedited, or would standard delivery be acceptable?
- ▶ Will you need this product invoiced by end of quarter, or can we deliver after end of quarter?
- ▶ I can get you a trial tomorrow—would that help, or would you prefer to wait for the shipping product to be delivered?

In short, you're attempting to assess how *desperate* your prospective customers are—how much they need you, relative to how much you need them. Overall, unless the vendor is the exclusive global source for a critical product, vendors usually need customers more than customers need vendors.

Unless the vendor is the exclusive global source for a critical product, vendors usually need customers more than customers need vendors.

Yet individual purchasers may be in different situations, either due to realities of short-term business or due to psychological anchoring. For example, you may need to pay exorbitant rates for an overnight courier instead of the U.S. Postal Service because of a business reality—you were unable to complete a contract until the very last minute. Alternatively, you may pay more for courier service because you've spent a lot of effort establishing the service contract for your company, and now feel compelled to use the service.

The stronger the balance of power is on your side versus on your customers' side, the better qualified the lead—because your position gives you the ability to resist naturally occurring customer tendencies to postpone purchase and argue price in search of "the best deal."

Summary: Don't waste time with people who can't buy from you—be sure to assess their interest, means, and cause to buy.

- ▶ Do they care about your business' offerings?
- ▶ Can they afford you?
- ▶ Do they have any external reasons to buy *now*?

Watch the Hands, Not the Mouth

Asking questions of prospective customers to determine their qualifications as leads has the advantage of being rapid. Unfortunately, it is also intrusive, which risks alienating valuable prospects, and may be inaccurate due to deliberate or inadvertent provision of incorrect information. People lie.

A different way of calculating proximity to purchase is to analyze customer behavior—specifically, response to marketing programs. What people are actually *doing* is more of a commit than what they're *saying*. This type of background analysis also has the advantages of being less intrusive and more scaleable than direct questioning. It's an automatable process, with effectively zero marginal costs—a perfect fit for entrepreneurial marketing and lead qualification.

There are three critical aspects to qualifying leads via analysis:

▸ Watch the hands, not the mouth

▸ Mechanics of data-gathering

▸ Mechanics of analysis—linear programming, database analysis

Watch the Hands, Not the Mouth

There are many ways of expressing the fundamental reality that ancillary *actions* are a better indicator of people's true intentions than are their expressed intentions. "Watch the hands, not the mouth," "Actions speak louder than words," "Walk the walk, don't just talk the talk," and other expressions all recognize that *physical actions show greater commitment than verbal statements.*

This doesn't necessarily indicate a deliberate intention on the part of prospective customers to mislead vendors. It's just that often prospects may not be in full conscious possession of the facts. They may have no idea that their divisional budget is about to be cut or have personal loans called—but at a "gut level" they're not comfortable committing to a purchase, because their subconscious has picked up many more cues and has figured out the conclusion. "Gut feel" is simply the collective set of subconscious impressions—and so action or inaction can actually express these hidden agendas. As the saying goes, "It's harder to lie with your feet than your mouth."

Specifically, marketing response actions, such as replying to or taking action on an e-mail solicitation, viewing a webinar, or attending a seminar represent a deepening of commitment with an associated benefit—an increase in the education level of your prospects. The additional benefit is not insignificant: A prospect expressing interest in your product prior to education isn't as qualified a prospect as one who maintains interest after education. In other words, if they learn more about who you are and what you do, and still don't run away, they're a great candidate for a sale.

Why is an educated prospect inherently more committed and better qualified? Not only has the prospect taken positive action to respond, deepening commitment, but also they are attracted to the actual product, not just your message and marketing.

For example, think about visiting a new restaurant. Prior to your visit,

There are many ways of expressing the fundamental reality that ancillary actions are a better indicator of people's true intentions than are their expressed intentions.

109

you're attracted to it because you're responding to the messaging—the promise created by good reviews and a great menu. If you return for a second visit, you're returning because the actuality of the restaurant lived up to its promise, though perhaps in different ways than advertised (better food, worse atmosphere).

In this vein, a good company will put its potential leads through several successively more involved marketing educational processes, and see what messages resonate, and which leads come out at the end. If the message and the product actuality are aligned, the resultant leads should be highly committed and educated—benefits which will accelerate and improve the ability of sales to close deals.

Mechanics of Data-Gathering

To perform scaleable analysis of customer response to marketing actions, it's critical to have a record of their answers. To understand what *you're* doing, you need a record of what *they* did.

Your goal is straightforward. In an ideal situation, you would have a simple table similar to the one on the next page.

Each row would represent one prospect—company, division, or individual, depending on the unit size in which your product is sold and the master index you choose to use to associate all marketing. For example, e-mail domain—the part to the right of the @ symbol in an e-mail address—is a relatively common index.

Each column would have two attributes: a date and a type, where "type" represented the marketing response level—for example, "e-mail," "webinar," "seminar," "postcard," and so forth.

In the final, right-most column, would be the total sales to that row over the period of time in question.

Every time a marketing program was run, the responses would be noted accordingly. Every time a sale was made, the sales total would be incremented appropriately. The net result would be a matrix ready for correlation analysis or linear programming optimization for maximum sales.

How do you actually know when individuals "responded"? Require registration. E-mail is a well-accepted request when asking for trials, whitepapers, webinar, or seminar registration (see prior chapter on Contact Capture), and makes domain as a master index an obvious mechanism.

Alternatively, you can use more involved tracking mechanisms, such as offer codes, tracking URLs and cookies (online), and referrers, to name a few. Just remember that the more complex or onerous to the end user, the less likely your system is to capture the data you need, effectively.

Master Index	E-Mail 1: Introduction		E-Mail 2: Whitepaper	
	Date	# Responses	Date	# Responses
real.com	13 Jan	0	12 Feb	5
vmware.com	13 Jan	4	12 Feb	3
hp.com	13 Jan	5	12 Feb	4
inktomi.com	13 Jan	7	12 Feb	7
smallco.com	13 Jan	2	12 Feb	1
SPC.com	13 Jan	6	12 Feb	3
SGI.com	13 Jan	8	12 Feb	4

Webinar: Intro		Seminar 1: Intro		Seminar 2: Technical		
Date	# Responses	Date	# Responses	Date	# Responses	Sales
10 Mar	0	12 Apr	5	24 May	0	$20,000
10 Mar	4	12 Apr	3	24 May	4	$30,000
10 Mar	5	12 Apr	4	24 May	5	$70,000
10 Mar	7	12 Apr	7	24 May	7	$40,000
10 Mar	2	12 Apr	1	24 May	2	$90,000
10 Mar	6	12 Apr	3	24 May	6	$10,000
10 Mar	8	12 Apr	4	24 May	8	$5,000

Mechanics of Analysis

So you have your table. Now what? The simplest approach to analysis is to qualify leads on a semi-qualitative basis. Append a weighted "score" to each contact, modified by age. For example, if response to e-mail is worth a "1," and the larger effort of attending a seminar is worth a "3," both minus 0.2 for each month each ages after three months, then anyone who has an interest score of greater than 5 (responded to five e-mails in a three-month period, or two e-mails and a seminar in three months, or two seminars within eight months) may be worth passing on to sales.

Note that the weighting may be qualitatively or quantitatively applied. On a qualitative basis, e-mail response "feels like" it takes less effort than a seminar response, would indicate less interest, and thus have a lower interest score of 1. On a quantitative basis, it should be possible to assign all responses equal weights initially, then run a regression analysis on the relative sales outcomes—the result of the algorithm should give you a relative weighting. This quantitative approach is suggested if you have a very wide range and high volume of marketing programs, high contact flow, and less ability to distinguish between commitment levels based on type of marketing program response.

Regardless of which approach you pick, do *something*—only then can you understand your customers.

Venture capitalists are famous for never saying "no," just "not yet"—because they correctly realize that the unqualified, time-wasting lead of today may be the overqualified lead of tomorrow, who you'd hate to offend.

Summary: Qualify leads via behavioral analysis, not just interviews.

- ▶ Watch what they do, not just what they say.
- ▶ Collect that data.
- ▶ Use some nonbiased mathematics to understand the data.

Parting Thought: On Firing Your Bad Leads

In the early 1990s, a consulting team that's now part of Mercer put forth a hypothesis that said, approximately, "some customers aren't worth having as customers." Their point was that some customers cost businesses more in support costs and management time than the customers contributed to the businesses in revenue.

Their solution: Fire the customers—raise fees until the customers are either profitable or leave.

Yet leads aren't customers—you can't raise fees on someone who isn't paying you anything yet, and moreover, their value isn't established. So it may make more sense to use the venture capital model. Venture capitalists are famous for never saying "no," just "not yet"—because they correctly realize that the unqualified, time-wasting lead of today may be the overqualified lead of tomorrow, whom you'd hate to offend.

So you must do a balancing act, focusing your efforts on the qualified leads, without losing the (currently) unqualified leads. How can you do this? Divide your marketing activities into zero-variable-cost and non-zero-variable-cost buckets. E-mail, for example, is close to zero cost per e-mail (once you've paid a fixed fee for your Internet connectivity or e-mail host). So sending an electronic newsletter to your leads, regardless of age of lead, is useful. You'll stay in touch. Conversely, a heavy photo-catalog costs several dollars each to produce and mail, above and beyond any one-time fixed cost of catalog creation. You should stop sending the catalog to any customer who hasn't purchased in some predetermined period of time—probably two catalog cycles.

You can further finetune the process by giving longer extensions of time to customers who might be worth more (for example, the customer who has a large budget, or who has previously purchased a lot from you stays on your catalog mailer longer without making a purchase than a prospect who has a low budget or who hasn't purchased much).

Over time, you won't be forced to "fire" your prospects—but you'll spend according to their worth, and people will "fire" themselves appropriately. So examine your marketing costs, and start stopping; use marketing to reward only those leads who reward you.

Chapter 7

Overcome Competition
Other People's Money ...
and Leads

"Those skilled in warfare move the enemy, and are not moved by the enemy."

—Sun-tzu, *The Art of War*

"The enemy of my enemy is my friend."

—Proverb

IF YOUR COMPETITOR'S MARKETING COSTS THEM MORE THAN IT COSTS YOU, you win. Having successfully generated awareness, captured contacts, filtered leads, and made sales, the next marketing challenge you need to consider is competition.

Given the amount of time and effort you've spent building your marketing programs and associated sales funnel, it's critical to protect your results from competitive theft. To remain successful, you must ensure that money you spent on finding need, building awareness, and capturing and qualifying contacts isn't lost to a prospect's decision to purchase from another company.

You will have *some* competitive losses. But even your competitive losses should contribute to your company's continued lead generation and sales dominance.

Poor managers spend a disproportionate amount of money attempting to out-shout their competition, somehow believing that by exposing prospective customers to a sufficient volume of marketing, regardless of the value (or lack of value) of that marketing to the recipients, they can brainwash the prospective customer into choosing a given product.

There is a lower-cost, more customer-friendly way to overcome competition. This chapter will provide you with a judo-like approach to competition, showing you ways to use your competition's efforts against them, regardless of their size. By the end of the chapter, you will understand how to leverage your competitors' market education efforts and spending, and build on *their* lead-generation efforts. Used correctly, your competitors can become some of *your* best sales and marketing allies.

Like Sun-tzu, you can move your competitors instead of being moved by them, by knowing how to implement the following tactics:

- ▶ **Follow the icebreaker:** Let your competition do the need location, initial education, and in some cases even lead qualification for you.

- ▶ **Use other people's leads:** Engage in hardball tactics such as calling on deals your competition lists as reference customers, modeling their collateral, and hiring their salespeople.

- ▶ **Dance with the elephants:** Partner with everyone, turning your environment into a competitor-less competition game.

Remember, what matters is *not* how you play the game; it's whether you win or lose.

Follow the Icebreaker: Compete via Comparison

Competitors can help you by assisting with *external-to-your-company* challenges, such as doing market education for you. Let *them* spend the time and money to teach customers about the need for your solution—then all you need to do is push against the competitor for the top position at the *end* of the sales cycle, spending your time with the customer talking about "who's better," not "why the customer needs this product."

Bad managers think that business competitors are their enemy—their primary opposition in lead generation. Those managers are wrong. Time, lack of market awareness, and customers who don't understand why you're worth spending money on all present more formidable challenges for an entrepreneurial marketer to overcome. If there's no market, everyone dies. Competition—who wins—is a secondary concern.

Like a fleet caught in an ice floe, your and your competitors' first concern should be survival against the elements—the market forces—and your secondary concern should be share or profitability relative to each other. Only after your market is well established, beyond hyper-growth and into maturity, should competition be an issue.

Only after your market is well established, beyond hyper-growth and into maturity, should competition be an issue.

So, like the fleet, you should leverage the efforts of your competition. Rather than spending your resources icebreaking at five miles per hour for the competitor three feet behind you, you should work in parallel, or even reverse positions—where *you* draft closely behind your competitor, saving your energy for a critical juncture when you can build on the market development work they've done.

Entrepreneurial managers understand how to follow the icebreaker by doing three things:

▶ Leverage the second mover advantage.

▶ Create contrast.

▶ Reset the agenda.

Leverage the Second-Mover Advantage

When is it a good thing to be the second person into the minefield, the second person to the dining table, or the second person into the water? When the first gets blown up, eats the poisoned curry, or realizes they're surrounded by sharks. Your competition can help you by testing the market for you—acting as a "royal taster" or "crash-test dummy," finding the hidden traps and successful marketing approaches so that *you* don't have to learn the painful and expensive way.

Being a second-mover isn't an intuitive strategy. Many business school classes teach the concept of the "first-mover advantage"—how being the first entrant into a market space can enable you to capture and hold dominant market share, disproportionate profits, and other business advantages.

But the truth is that the first mover often fails. Business history is filled with examples of companies who spent millions (or hundreds of millions) of dollars in market development, only to succumb to second- (or third-, or fourth-, or twenty-ninth-) mover competitors. Before Google was worth billions of dollars, there were search engines Altavista, Hotbot, Yahoo, DirectHit, AskJeeves, and hundreds of others. Before Hotmail, Juno was spending tens of millions of dollars in advertising, promoting their free e-mail service. Windowed software was first widely available on the Apple Macintosh, years before Microsoft introduced the feature. Betamax format videocassette recorders were first to market and technically superior to VHS. The list goes on and on. To this day, large companies like Cisco Systems and Microsoft often wait until a market is firmly established before entering through acquisition of a smaller company (see, for example, the streaming media industry).

So why do later entrants win? Commonalities to successful second-movers are markets with high initial barriers to introduction, but low subsequent switching costs.

For example, the first genetically modified food company faced enormous legal and legislative approval barriers. Yet once they'd spent the money to win approval, they'd set precedent—and companies following similar development paths faced a much cheaper, quicker route to market.

Similarly, educating the market about the value and use of new products is a long and arduous process. Consider the digital video recorder (DVR). Ten years after being founded, TiVo, the company that introduced the DVR, was still spending millions of dollars in market education, answering the question, "What is a DVR and why do I need one?" and was still unprofitable. Unfortunately for them, at that 10-year point, as the educated market was reaching sufficient size to be profitable, other better-positioned manufacturers such as Hughes/Comcast started introducing their own DVRs. Once educated, switching barriers for consumers in both circumstances were low—and so second-movers could usurp first entrants.

So what can an entrepreneurial manager do to leverage these competitive dynamics for efficient marketing? Ask yourself the following questions:

> ▶ What are the barriers to entry in this industry? Are they related to market education, legislation, execution, or technology? If the barriers are nontechnical, such as government regulations, let others overcome the barriers for you. Be the *second* leaf-blower user in town, or the second liquor store, after the first such business changes the regulations.

> ▶ What are the switching barriers for consumers? Can they move easily to your product? If so, how do you plan to move them—and how can you make it difficult for them to move back? (See the last section of this chapter.)

Educating the market about the value and use of new products is a long and arduous process.

117

▶ Who are the leaders in this market? Why?

▶ Who are their customers?

Then use the information you've gathered to create contrast and reset the agenda.

Create Contrast

Competitors provide great contrast, and contrast is essential for an entrepreneurial manager, because it saves you marketing time and effort.

Competitors provide great contrast, and contrast is essential for an entrepreneurial manager, because it saves you marketing time and effort. Without comparison or contrast, customers don't know how to value your offering. Sure, your business may save them time and money, but what's your offering really *worth*? If customers don't understand how poorly off they are—what "bad" really is—at a visceral level, it takes significantly more marketing educational effort to convince them that your product offering is "good," and worth the price asked for it.

With contrast, customer education and choice becomes easier. It's simpler to differentiate and explain the value of an off-road vehicle by comparing it to a standard sedan—and if you choose your points of comparison carefully, you'll always look better than your competition. For example, sociological studies have shown that when seeking to differentiate for advantage in social circumstances, individuals seek to pair themselves with highly differentiated partners. In other words, when you're trying to appear more attractive to others, you "hang out" with your uglier friend(s). When trying to seem smarter, you consciously or unconsciously surround yourself with folks who aren't as strong intellectually. Outsiders observing you will instinctively take the psychological shortcut of local comparison, and correspondingly give you higher value than you objectively deserve. You'll look better and smarter than you are.

So how can competition help you? When you're being compared on price, stand next to the expensive competitor. When you're being compared on technology, stand next to the stupid competitor—where you can translate "stand next to" as "be featured in a product comparison with" (a media comparison or one you published).

There are limits to the use of comparison. It's not without risk—the two biggest risks being *inadvertent grouping* and *publicity*.

Grouping occurs when you add too many comparison points with insufficient differentiation. Standing next to one or two dumb kids makes you look like the smart one in the class. Standing next to 50 dumb kids, you look like you're part of the group. Be sure to choose your comparison points carefully, and deploy selectively. Contrast only as necessary.

Publicity is the second risk. Excessive use of explicit comparison can build awareness of your competition. Only use explicit contrast if the customer initiates the comparison—if they name the competitor. Otherwise you're doing your competitor the favor of introducing them to your customer.

Whenever possible, use implicit comparison—for example, don't say "unlike competitor BigCo, our product is super-fast." Instead, simply say, "Our product is the fastest of its kind," and let the competitor implicitly appear slow.

Of course, everyone is better at something, and everything has value in some way. As software engineers sometimes remark, "it's not a bug, it's a feature." There's value in being the ugliest as well as the prettiest kid at the dance. So it's important to use contrast in conjunction with agenda-setting.

Reset the Agenda

Everyone is better at something—and the third way to leverage your competitors is to take advantage of *their* customer education efforts to further *your* customer sales.

For example, imagine a situation where your competitor has proven the market for automobiles. They've spent money explaining the advantages of having an automobile over having a horse or riding a trolley. They've explained the concepts of tires and gasoline. At great expense, they've made a large portion of the possible set of automobile purchasers aware of the product family.

Now imagine you enter this market with a set of marketing activities around a point of contrast. Your argument? What matters most in buying an automobile is color, and you're the only producer of colored vehicles. Or perhaps what matters most is gas mileage, or soft suspension, or repair record—in any case, you're the only provider of this benefit. Don't know your points of positive differentiation? Ask your existing customers why *they* purchased your product, and exploit that possibly hidden value. You're the best to *someone* for *some* reason—and that someone probably isn't alone in the marketplace.

By spending your marketing dollars selectively on changing your customers' perceptions, instead of creating initial awareness, you can dramatically increase the efficiency of your efforts. Avis was able to dramatically increase their market share over Hertz in the rental car market by taking the market awareness that Hertz had created ("Rental cars exist, are respectable, and are useful airport-based services for business travelers *and* casual travel-

By spending your marketing dollars selectively on changing your customers' perceptions, instead of creating initial awareness, you can dramatically increase the efficiency of your efforts.

ers") and resetting the agenda with relatively minimal expenditure ("it's about service—we try harder"). Avis remained behind Hertz, but leaped ahead of other agencies—and their return on lead-generation investment was substantially better than if they'd attempted to emulate Hertz's spending.

In short, entrepreneurial managers believe in standing on the shoulders of giants. Let your competitor break the ice for you.

Competitors can help you by doing market education, tilling the ground for you to seed, so that you can then position yourself simply by comparison.

Summary: Competitors can help you by doing market education, tilling the ground for you to seed, so that you can then position yourself simply by comparison.

▶ **Leverage second-mover advantages:** Avoid the mistakes your competition made, be more focused more efficiently.

▶ **Create contrast:** Save your marketing dollars by finding audiences your competition has already spent the effort to educate, then saying, "We solve the same issues as [competitor X], only better in these ways."

▶ **Reset the agenda:** Save your marketing dollars by finding audiences your competition has already spent the effort to educate, then supplying "the solution."

Use Other People's Leads: Compete via Incrementalism

Competitors can help you by taking care of *internal-to-your-company* challenges, such as building infrastructure and doing market research for you. They create collateral, train salespeople, and find out which companies or people are buying your type of offerings—all efforts that you can take and use.

Bad managers feel compelled to reinvent the wheel. Every program, bit of collateral, or discovered lead must originate from within their team, so that they can claim credit. They're willing to spend the same millions of dollars that their competitors already spent, just to claim they've "discovered" the same prospect company contacts, markets that work, and accounts ready to buy.

Good managers are efficient. They recognize that it's far easier and cheaper to buy a copy of a map than to invest in remapping the terrain themselves. Good entrepreneurial managers act ethically but aggressively, and leverage their competitors' marketing investments and efforts in three ways, as follows:

- ▶ Modeling their collateral.
- ▶ Hiring their salespeople.
- ▶ Calling on their accounts.

Modeling Their Collateral

If a competitor has put together a customer presentation that explains the industry, product family, and value of the product to the customer, that's great for you. Assuming there's no copyrighted or proprietary material—that the presentation is public and contains publicly available data—you have the foundation for *your* presentation.

Your competitor has just done what would have taken you hours to weeks of work, or cost you high fees for an outside consultant to create. So take their presentation, and redo it with better graphics, additional data (so that it's clear you're more of an expert in the product space), and a bias toward your product's strengths.

Most prospective customers will willingly share competitive presentations that aren't proprietary, so ask your customers for your competitors' presentations if you know your customers have already seen and have copies of those presentations—and then ask that your customers sign a nondisclosure agreement (NDA) before viewing your presentation.

Now, ask the customer where the competitor's presentation *wasn't* compelling, and what they'd really want to have seen instead. Then build in what they've told you they want.

Note that there's a fine line between looking like a copycat or wannabe after a competitor has set the agenda, versus delaying your presentation to really show the prospective customer a more professional presentation and greater depth of knowledge. Both positions exist—so understand which one you are in *before* you present to the customer.

If a competitor has put together a customer presentation that explains the industry, product family, and value of the product to the customer, that's great for you.

Hiring Their Salespeople

Who knows the market and product space better than your *competitor's* best salespeople? Your competitor has been kind enough to train them for you, let them build their personal knowledge and contacts, and let them understand the strengths and weaknesses of your competitor. Sales is the lifeblood of any company, and typically a comparatively small part of the sales team generates the majority of sales. Take those people, and your competitor will be struggling while you grow.

How do you find their best salespeople? Ask your customers which salespeople they dealt with, and your customers' preferred representative. Interview other employees of your competitors. Hire your competitor's head of sales, or director of their strongest sales territory, and have them point out the other people you need to hire.

Why should the best salespeople leave your competitor to join you? It's about the money and the autonomy. You can offer them space to grow as you take share from your competitor. As long as your product is good, sales will follow the path of greatest reward for least effort—and you have a great marketing and sales-lead-generation team.

Beware—act honorably. Don't steal intellectual property. If a salesperson built contacts on his or her own time, that's fine, but beware of database theft; it's traceable and prosecutable.

Calling On Their Accounts

It's easier to convert customers than to create customers. So call on your competitors' accounts. They've already been identified as valuable leads and have been partially educated; now, they're ready to buy, and it's at the end of the consideration process that substitutions can be made.

Call on your competitors' accounts. They've already been identified as valuable leads and have been partially educated.

So, find the customer. Read your competitor's customer success stories and press releases. Hire teams to follow their salespeople. Attend their events or hang out at their trade-show booth and write down names. Be an annoyance to your competitors! Then, convert the customer. Were they aware of your solution? What's the barrier to purchasing your solution instead of the competitor's? Remove the barrier and sell.

Of course, this must all be done *while* building your own new accounts. You don't want to distract your whole company and lose focus—so this competitive conversion program must be created as an isolated SWAT team, driven by one senior sales or marketing person, rewarded accordingly, with top-level access to executives (you).

Call on the customers listed in your competitors' press releases, and deliver better solutions at lower prices. Read your competitors' success stories, call on the listed customers, and deliver better results. Follow the competitors into their accounts, while building your own list of customers. Never let up on the pressure.

Summary: Competitors can help you by doing market infrastructure creation, building marketing materials, training salespeople, and overcoming initial customer barriers to sales—all of which you can then take and use for your business.

- ▶ **Model their materials:** Use the marketing presentations, charts, graphs, and research they've done, recast to support why *your* business is superior.

- ▶ **Hire their salespeople:** Use the trained, skilled, relationship-owning salespeople they've created… to sell *your* offerings.

- ▶ **Call on their customers:** Don't spend time persuading customers they need your type of solution. Instead, go to the customers that have had their barriers to sales overcome by your competitor, and are now believers in your type of business. Then spend the minimal incremental effort needed to prove *your* business is the superior provider.

Dance with the Elephants: Compete via Partnerships

Competitors can help you by eliminating each other as threats: fighting with each other so that you can gain share. In fact, the only thing worse than being out in a market with many potential competitors is being in a market with only one. When there are several, they distract each other.

Bad managers try to take on the world. They believe that the only way to defeat the competition is to challenge every competitor head on, on every aspect, simultaneously.

Good managers recognize that the difference between a competitor and a partner may only be a timing issue, or a matter of which division in a company has ascendancy at a given moment.

Entrepreneurial managers would rather be in a market with several evenly matched competitors, as they follow three steps to improve their own lead generation using their competitors' effort.

Entrepreneurial managers:

- ▶ Get out of the middle.
- ▶ Point the competitors at each other.
- ▶ Work the unattended customers.

The only thing worse than being out in a market with many potential competitors is being in a market with only one.

Get Out of the Middle

Most companies have several areas of business—several areas on which to focus. Each area has its own points of differentiation—as previously discussed, your lead-generation efforts will already have been focused on differentiating yourself from at least one area. If you're in lawn care, are you a tree specialist, garden specialist, flower specialist?

But if you're sufficiently differentiated, an argument could be made that you're complementary to at least part of any specific competitor. So a customer who wanted a full solution should be considering a joint implementation of both product sets, yours and your competitors'. For example, a competitor of yours that is focused on gardens needs your tree expertise.

Your first task is to successfully make this complementary argument—to partner with your potential competitor. Seem unlikely? RealNetworks initially partnered with Microsoft in the streaming media space. IBM and EMC partnered in a software distribution area, even as other divisions competed over storage. Netscape and Yahoo (among others) partnered against AOL even as the companies competed in other ways. "Coopetition," the term coined by Ray Noorda (founder of Novell) reflects the duopoly of relationship that can occur even if the companies remain in competition—and your task is to initially remove as much of the competitive appearance as possible. Shake hands with your competitor with the hand that isn't training a gun on them.

When successful, repeat the process with each of your competitors. In an industry where everyone is fighting over "Product A" your goal is to differentiate yourself and contrast or reposition as "Product B" (as previously discussed), and partner with everyone, outside of the fight over A. For example, if the current competition is over who could provide the fastest product, strive to be the one company providing the best support, or best user experience—orthogonal to the others, but just as customer-critical. In the garden care example, everyone needs the tree guys.

Point Your Competitors at Each Other

Your second task is to invert your complementary logic when talking to your competitive partners, and emphasize to each how much more competitive they are with each other than they are with you.

Your task is to dramatically escalate the competition over "Product A," while you're partnered with each on solutions in the "Product B" space. In the garden care example, point out that they're all garden guys, competing for the same customer.

To maintain the relationship, you need to continue to fuel both sides of the relationship.

▶ On the positive side, be sure your connection to each competitive company provides some value to them. Refer to joint deals you've done (regardless of who made the introduction—ideally, let them do the intros). Feature them in some press releases touting the relationship. Build a demonstration that they can use showing your products working together (the extra publicity this use will bring you is worth the small investment). Do enough to keep them interested in you as a partner, keep them away from others as partners, and keep them from choosing to pursue internal competitive development.

▶ On the negative side, be sure your competitor remains *competitive* with your other competitors. Continue to provide each of your competitors with appropriate information to feed the friction—highlighting every competitive loss, and encouraging them in hostile actions.

If successful, you'll still be out of the middle—and the other kids on the playground will be fighting so hard with each other that they won't notice you eating their lunch.

Work the Unattended

Your third and final task is to build your position while your competitors are fighting. Ideally, you'll have chosen your position for growth and rapid development, and your competitors will be fighting over a mature area anyway. (This is not unlikely; it's easier to fight over a small field of mature corn than a large field of sprouts. People lack vision to forward-invest. Think about sales of housing—there's still more competition for houses in a decaying suburb than for land in undeveloped areas.)

Your own position can be built tactically and strategically. Tactically, get *your* presence into jointly owned customer accounts. As was the situation with list recapture in the prior chapters, once introduced to a customer, you can build your *own* relationship with that customer.

Strategically, work to ensure the customer views your "Product B" aspects as being the value in the joint solution. Make your competition the replaceable half of the partnership in the customers' eyes. Commoditize their part of the value chain—assist in value migration to your area.

Again, this is a well-demonstrated concept. In the software space, Microsoft most famously commoditized IBM, convincing customers that software was more important (and worth more) than hardware—but in case you thought the lesson was learned and not repeatable, Checkpoint partnered with Sun for distribution of the Checkpoint firewall, and did the same thing that Microsoft did with IBM again 25 years later. EMC did the same in the furniture business, moving from competing on supplying racks to letting that area commoditize while they supplied computer hardware.

So focus on shifting your customers' views. Keep whispering to your customer that the tree work is really what matters. Then wave goodbye as your customer fires the garden guys.

Summary: Competitors can help you by keeping other competitors from hurting you—if you can keep them focused on beating each other, they're not thinking about exterminating you.

▶ **Get out of the middle:** Be competitive with only a part of your competitors' business, even as you are a useful complement and partner to another part.

▶ **Point your competitors at each other:** Emphasize and amplify the threat of each competitor to each other competitor, while minimizing your participation in the battle.

▶ **Work the unattended:** Make friends with the customers while the competitors are distracted.

Parting Thought: The Best Defense Is a Good Defense

Even as you attempt to implement the tactics described above, your competitors will be attempting the same tactics against you.

It's a fatal mistake to assume your competition hasn't read the same books you have. Even as you attempt to implement the tactics described above, your competitors will be attempting the same tactics against you. So be prepared to defend yourself. If you're prepared, the winner will be the best implementer—the most effective marketer—and you'll be fine.

So how do you prepare? Sometimes the best defense isn't just having a good offense, it's also having a good defense.

Do four things to defend yourself:

▶ **Be focused:** As an entrepreneur, you are the *best* solution to a specific problem. So don't try to be everything to everyone. If you're the best lawn care company in town, but there are many competitors, focus on your strength and tout it: "The *best* lawn care." Don't expand into tree-trimming, shrubs, or other aspects of landscaping, instead, partner for that. Be the best or quit.

▸ **Create loyalty:** Listen to your customers, and give them what they need in order to create super-loyal reference accounts. You need a solid foundation of customers who will testify to your "best-ness," and won't be wooed away by competitors. Publicize only these best accounts in your marketing materials, and ask them to explain why you're the best. Reward loyalty. Don't give people a reason to switch.

▸ **Build awareness of you:** Spend on awareness of *you* at least as much as on awareness of your solution value. In other words, if there's lots of competition, let the others spend on customer education as to why they *need* lawn care. You spend on why *your* service is the *best* for lawn care. Be specific and egocentric. *Your* name and unique benefit are what need to stand out to break through the noise of marketing.

▸ **Create friction, or lock-in:** As discussed in prior chapters, make it annoying for your customers to switch away from you, by maintaining their preferences and profiles, obtaining longer-term contracts, offering loyalty programs like "frequent-flyer points," and so forth.

Spend 80 percent of your time on being the best—and 20 percent of your time misleading your competition.

Spend 80 percent of your time on being the best—and 20 percent of your time misleading your competition, spreading rumors within the competitive group (not with your customers) that you're about to invest millions of dollars in television advertising, or buy a giant warehouse on another continent, or whatever it takes to worry and mislead your competition into spending time and effort pursuing useless activities to "keep up" with your (nonexistent) plans.

As Douglas Adams said, "Don't Panic." The person who keeps their head when all around are losing theirs wins in the end.

Part Three

Reviewing

Chapter 8

Retain and Expand Customer Relationships
Avoiding the One-Night Stand

"I will praise any man that will praise me."

—William Shakespeare, *Antony and Cleopatra*

IF YOU ONLY MAKE ONE SALE PER CUSTOMER, YOU'RE ACTUALLY WORKING for your competition. It is well documented that the cost of acquiring a new customer outweighs the cost of sales to an existing customer. Yet too often entrepreneurs get caught up in the thrill of the hunt. They make a sale and move on, failing to secure customer loyalty. The result? Customers make subsequent purchases from competitors, who need to spend far less effort on marketing education (as discussed in Chapter 6). They win, you lose on costs *and* sales—and eventually, when you run out of customer deals to hunt, your business dies.

So as an entrepreneurial marketer, you must be both a hunter and a farmer. You must hunt, spending effort to get a customer, and farm, cultivating the relationship. If you're a born hunter, get a farmer as a partner, and vice versa. Having invested in educating, obtaining, and defending sales to customers, it is critical that you take steps ensuring that you keep your customers.

This chapter will discuss the value of and tactics involved in forging mature customer relationships that *also* generate incremental sales. You'll learn when it's appropriate to invest in a long-term relationship with a customer and when it's not, how to get customers to pay *you* more to stay with you, and how making them look good can make you look good.

You'll learn how to:

▶ **Know when long-term is good**: Assess the value of customer relationships.

▶ **Get customers to pay more to stay safe**: Build a relationship via premium support, by invoking "fear of stick."

▶ **Make heroes**: Build a relationship via creation of customer champions, by invoking the "lure of the carrot."

Just remember, the thrill of the chase is all very fine—and it's nice to get a prospect you've chased and hunted as a new customer—but it's keeping them a customer in the long term that ensures the success of your business.

Know When Long-Term Is Good

There are businesses where transactional relationships are more efficient. But most of the time, the cost of a sale to an existing customer is less than the cost of acquiring a new customer.

Sometimes it *is* OK to "love 'em and leave 'em." There *are* businesses where transactional relationships are more efficient. But most of the time, the cost of a sale to an existing customer is less than the cost of acquiring a new customer.

In addition, the *lifetime* value of the customer—the amount they'll spend with you over the entire time they'll buy from you—is usually high enough to justify the effort and expense involved in keeping them as your customer.

So how can you tell when a long-term relationship is a good idea? There are three aspects of the cost of a customer that you'll need to understand:

▶ Cost of a sale to an existing customer versus to a new customer.

▶ Lifetime value of a customer.

▶ When transactional makes sense.

Cost of Sale to an Existing versus New Customer

New customers are expensive to acquire. Consider the relative costs of a sale to a current customer versus the costs of a sale to a new customer. There are three kinds of costs: transactional costs, overhead costs, and acquisition costs.

Transactional (variable) costs are those that occur *each time* you do business with your customer. In most businesses, transactional costs are about the same for new customers and current customers. For example, it doesn't cost the dentist any more to examine your teeth the thirty-fifth time than it does to examine them the first time.

Overhead (fixed) costs are those that occur only *periodically* in the history of your relationship with the customer—and overhead costs of new customers are much larger than those of existing customers. For example, the first time you visit a dentist, they must assess your general condition, obtain and process your medical history and insurance, and familiarize you with their practice, policies, and procedure. The thirty-fifth time you visit, none of that overhead is necessary—it's already in place. So a dentist with an established practice is spending far less on overhead than a dentist seeing all new patients.

Acquisition (fixed) costs are those that occur only *once* in the history of your relationship with the customer. Only new customers have acquisition costs. If your awareness and contact capture programs resulted in your spending $1,000 to obtain ten new customers who each spend $250 with you per purchase, those customers have an implicit cost to you of $100 each per purchase (leaving you with a profit of only $150). If those customers become repeat customers, and visit you five times instead of once, their per-purchase cost is effectively $20 instead of $100, leaving you with a profit of $230 per purchase, and an overall higher profit. Would it be worth a $5-per-purchase discount for you to keep those customers? Absolutely, as it only raises their per-purchase cost to $25, versus the $100 per-purchase cost of a one-purchase customer.

So it's clear that in situations where you have substantive per-customer initial overhead or acquisition costs, once you have a customer, it's worth keeping this client around.

Lifetime Value of a Customer

All customers are not equal. As can be seen in the prior example, you'd rather have a customer who visited you ten times than one who visited once—even if the ten-time visitor spent only half as much per visit as the single-time visitor.

Lifetime value of a customer refers to this calculation of total amount of dollars your customer will give you over the life of your relationship with them. In a conservative calculation, this value could just be the cash they actually spend with you; in a more broad interpretation, this value could also include the marketing dollars they save you by recruiting other customers.

It's clear that in situations where you have substantive per-customer initial overhead or acquisition costs, once you have a customer, it's worth keeping this client around.

So assess your customers on lifetime value. If you keep records of your customers (by last name, order ID number, or referral as discussed in Chapter 2), check their average value. How many times do they visit? What do they spend, on average? Can you tell what profile of customer is likely to match which spending pattern? (For example, do people in one part of town spend more? Do men spend more than women?)

Once you have a pattern, change your marketing. Target your marketing more at people who fit your high-value profile, ask your high-lifetime-value customers what would make them stay with you, and offer rewards accordingly.

Target your marketing more at people who fit your high-value profile, ask your high-lifetime-value customers what would make them stay with you, and offer rewards accordingly.

When Transactional Makes Sense

There are times when repeat business doesn't matter. Are your customers all of roughly equal lifetime value and minimal acquisition costs? Do they have minimal viral impact, spreading word of your business to few others? If so, it's not worth your time to develop a relationship with them. Spend as little marketing as possible on them and extract the maximum sales from them.

For example, consider certain types of new car buyers. If you're over 70 years old and buying a car for cash, there's little incentive for a dealer to invest in you. The odds are that you won't buy many more cars from them, won't influence many others to buy cars from them, and probably won't return to the showroom after buying this car. The relationship is thus almost purely transactional in nature. As a car dealership owner, you'd want to invest less in marketing to that purchasing segment, and more to people early in their car-buying life, with many colleagues of similar age.

Don't engage in illegal discriminatory behavior—but don't waste your time spending extra effort building relationships with customers who can't return the favor. If you have a customer who's constantly calling your support lines, never buys much, and otherwise costs you lots without returning much, treat them differently—for example, they should reach your answering machine, whereas your high-value customers might be given your cell phone number.

Summary: How do you know when a long-term customer relationship is worthwhile? It is when you have a customer who will make you more than they'll cost you if you spend more to keep them.

▶ **Costs:** Maintain low ongoing overhead costs relative to higher acquisition and startup costs.

▶ **Lifetime value:** Keep a high overall transactional spend value, or reputational value, with you.

▶ **Caution:** Beware of high-cost, low-value customers, and don't spend more than they're worth.

Get Customers to Pay More to Stay Safe

Since the early days of drayage, it has been said that you can motivate customers with reward or punishment—in the case of a cart mule, "carrot and stick." This concept translates well into today's business world. If you can protect people from punishment, you motivate them to work with you. Job security, via "safe" purchase decisions, is a form of protection.

Consider: In the late twentieth century it was frequently said, "No one was ever fired for buying IBM products." While a slight exaggeration, the statement illustrates the value customers place on your product being the safe choice when purchasing. Think about it: As a buyer choosing between two products, would you rather have the one that *might* be slightly better, or the one that *certainly* won't result in your being fired if it doesn't perform as advertised?

Risk, also known as "fear of a career blunder," is the psychological equivalent of "the stick" for many customers. Since any new purchase involves an element of risk, it is important to *minimize* that risk for your products, while maximizing the appearance of such risk for competing products. Most people are risk-averse when it comes to their careers. Thus, *you can forge customer relationships by helping them alleviate risk: helping them to avoid the stick.*

Since any new purchase involves an element of risk, it is important to minimize that risk for your products, while maximizing the appearance of such risk for competing products.

Premium support—the idea of customers paying you more so that you can be there when they need you—is also becoming a well-accepted concept. Yet there's a basic set of "necessary" reassurances that you should provide every customer for free, or you'll be perceived as excessively greedy.

So what's the correct spectrum of risk minimizers to offer your customer? They fall into three areas as follows:

▶ Basic paperwork.

▶ Going the extra mile.

▶ Pay to play.

Basic Paperwork

Putting promises on paper makes people feel better. Not only does this approach tend to clarify exactly what's being promised, but also in today's increasingly litigious business climate, having the signed contract with specified obligations makes customers feel more protected. Recourse is an escape hatch.

So what should you promise? Ask your customers what they fear—then listen to their answers, and quantify your response. Common fears and responses include some of the following:

▶ **Service and support:** Customers want to know that if they have trouble on their project, you'll be there for them. So specify a level of support—a service level agreement (SLA). State that your product won't break more than once every hundred years. State that you'll be reachable by phone within 60 minutes of their leaving a message, any time of day or night, any day of the year. State that you'll help resolve their problem, regardless of the cause (for example, some travel agencies will guarantee your flights, so that if your originally booked carrier has troubles, you can fly any other airline). State that if their lawn dies, you'll reseed it. Make sure your customer feels protected.

▶ **Costs and prices:** Customers want to know that they won't have overpaid. Specify a minimum level of cost savings for them, or a price guarantee. For example, many stores offer guarantees for 30 days on their goods—find a lower price, and the store will refund the difference or more. Some retailers offer savings guarantees, wherein they'll cover the difference or more if their product doesn't *save* you money.

▶ **Company viability:** Customers want to know that your business will be around to honor the former promises. Specify what they'll get if that isn't true. For example, many software companies place their source code in escrow for big customers. If the software company folds, the big customers get the code, so that they can continue to use and maintain the product. In extreme cases, the customer may have rights to your entire business—for example, Yahoo took ownership warrants in Google, so that if the company failed, Yahoo would have a significant say in the disposal of assets. In the case of smaller companies, viability guarantees may take the form of a posted bond and coverage agreement—so that if your business fails, your customer is still guaranteed that they'll get service for the next X amount of months or years from a covering company.

Of course, these assurances should be part of a trade. Would-be competitors should be held to the same standards that you're offering, and your customer should offer *quid pro quo*. If you make these assurances to them, they should make similar assurances to you about participating in your marketing by offering to endorse you, introduce you to other colleagues, or make some minimum number of purchases from you in the future.

Going the Extra Mile

The next step in creating a sense of safety in your customer is to deliver on *more* than your promises and assurances. Even bad situations can yield good customer relations and marketing outcomes. Companies understand that products may fail—often through unpreventable or unforeseen circumstances. *Your reaction* will determine whether your customer relationship improves or degrades. Being proactive and over-delivering on your stated, paper commitment will yield the best results.

For example, data-storage equipment vendor EMC faced a situation where one of their storage devices failed—not because of anything EMC did, but rather because the unit was physically dropped during a construction move. By the letter of their service agreement, EMC would have been within their rights to demand that the customer purchase a new unit—and wait in line for one with other requestors. Data restoration would also have been the customer's problem. Yet EMC went out of their way to locate and deliver a new unit, and assist the customer in restoring their data center to fully operational status.

EMC's action clearly validated the customer's trust in the safety of purchasing EMC equipment. But this "extra mile" concept applies to all sizes of businesses—from auto repair shops offering free "drop off" taxi service, to cleaners re-cleaning your shirts for free after the shirts land in a mud puddle as you leave the store.

So how can *you* create a similar relationship with your customers, and use it to support your marketing efforts?

▶ Gain clear agreement on and commitment to the escalation plans among all the employees in your business. For example, EMC's CEO was notified of the incident within 24 hours of it occurring—faster than the customer's CEO. An EMC executive was on site shortly thereafter. The lowest-level support person wasn't afraid to call the biggest boss. How accessible are *you*?

▶ After such an occurrence, while your customer is still grateful, ask for marketing support. After all, you saved their backside—would they be willing to publicize your support to other colleagues, or externally via an endorsement?

Reward begets reward. What goes around comes around—and builds loyalty.

Pay to Play

The last step in creating a sense of safety in your customer is to put in physical insurance that you'll deliver on your promises and assurances. As a customer, even if you're covered by paper guarantees and demonstrated commitment, it's reassuring to have a champion by your side—a dedicated resource, expert in the product you just purchased, chartered with making it (and you) successful.

Customers recognize the value of a dedicated expert, and will pay for one.

Customers recognize the value of a dedicated expert, *and will pay for one*. Whether this expert is you, available 24 hours a day, 7 days a week by cellular phone, or whether this person is an outside agency that you've trained and hired to answer your calls (e.g., a nurse screening calls for a physician), you can ask for appropriate extra payment if you can explain to your customers why this extra service will save them more than they're paying. You'll need to market the extra service as much as the original service—but it will save you customer-retention spending in the long term.

Summary: How do you increase customer retention via prevention of negative situations? Offer customer support.

- ▶ **Paperwork:** A relatively free way to reduce risk for your customers.
- ▶ **Going the extra mile:** Exceed your customers' expectations.
- ▶ **Pay to play:** You can extract a small additional profit for their greater comfort.

Make Heroes

Success breeds success. Selling a product that makes your customer more successful is good for both of you. In the "carrot and stick" analogy, helping your customers be successful is akin to offering them a carrot—it's a reward, a positive reinforcement for working with you.

Moreover, successful customers—both individual purchasers and their employers, if any—are financially and politically better positioned and more motivated to spread the word of your product's value through the rest of the company and industry.

Consider: If the recently promoted Vice President attributes much of their success to your product, you'll obtain more would-be emulators than if your product is grudgingly used (and not endorsed) by an individual clerk in the mailroom. The more influence your customer champion can wield on your behalf, the more successful they can make you.

So be a king-maker. It's easier than you might think. There are three well-established techniques for making your customers successful.

▶ Provide proof of their brilliance.

▶ Make them famous.

▶ Work with them.

Provide Proof of Their Brilliance

Your customers will be judged by your results—so *to create a hero, create and publicize results.* Did that party turn out well? At some level, conscious or subconscious, credit will go to the caterer. Does that suit look great? Credit the tailor or dry cleaner. Are the photos fantastic? Credit your camera maker and salesperson who sold it to you. As a business owner, you are *always* a part of your customers' successes (or failures), like it or not. So why not go the extra step, explicitly taking on some responsibility for the customer, and helping them demonstrate their brilliance to those observing their purchase decision.

As a business owner, you are always a part of your customers' successes (or failures), like it or not.

Specifically, you need to provide your customer with:

▶ **Planning:** Whether your customer is an individual or a company, they need to understand how using your business will affect others around them. Will your house painting for them potentially cause noise for the neighbors? Will your financial planning for them take time out of their workday, or possibly make them late for child-care pickup? Will your software installation for their team raise security concerns in their IT group? Your challenge as an entrepreneurial marketer is to put yourself not only in the customers' shoes, but in the shoes of those surrounding your customers, and advise your customers on how to plan accordingly.

▶ **Successful implementation:** Once your plan is in place, you must deliver according to plan for your customers. This includes successful and on-time delivery of your product or service as advertised. If you promise not to disturb the neighbors by working only during certain hours, stick to that plan!

▶ **Proof of success:** Having provided your customers with a success, cement that win. Document your success in reportable form. Did your business save a company money? Provide a one-page summary or two-bar chart showing them how much they would have spent versus how much they actually spent—for example, how much you saved them. Did your business make someone healthier or more financially secure? Deliver them a note of congrats with an article that they can show their friends, showing how their choice to use your business made them healthier or more secure. Did that house-painting job go particularly well? Show off your success. Survey the neighbors, and see what they say! From indirect proof such as articles showing that house painting adds value and longevity to the property, to direct proof measuring how much they saved by buying from your business versus others, your goal is to validate your customers' choice of *you*.

Don't wait. You know why your business helps people. Show your customers what you know. Don't stop marketing just because you made one sale. Help them feel good.

Make Them Famous

Having results is good, but as is the case with your business itself, publicizing your results—generating awareness of your chosen customer, your champion or "hero"—is the secret to success.

So, just as you would market your business, market your hero to their company or friends, and their company or friends to the industry or larger target audience. Touting others' success is a more effective way of getting awareness than touting your own success. Customers view third-party endorsements less suspiciously than self-endorsement. Your customer saying "you're a great business!" is more believable proof of greatness to others than you saying "I'm a great business!"

Your customer saying "you're a great business!" is more believable proof of greatness to others than you saying "I'm a great business!"

Marketing your hero can take several forms, *intrinsic* or *extrinsic* to the actual person you've chosen. The *intrinsic* approach to hero-making involves marketing the value of the *individual*—turning your customer into the expert who will endorse you.

How can you do this? Showcase your chosen customer as an industry expert, and promote this idea to their company or friends. Their friends or company may not have realized it until you started explaining it, but your chosen hero is *actually* a brilliant expert on (for example) assessing the best automobile repair services. As the vendor, you're *honored* that this renowned expert has chosen *your* service, and you'd be thrilled to quote them in your marketing literature. In fact, as a vendor, you'll even discount some future services for that quote—thus proving your hero's value.

In this situation, you win because the (now) expert endorses you; your hero wins because their value or esteem rises among their friends or company. See how it works? Marketing creates reality.

Alternatively, the *extrinsic* approach involves marketing the value of the individual's *results*.

How can you do this? Showcase your customers' results, explaining to their friends and company how your hero saved or made millions of dollars. This is a common tactic when marketing diet plans—where heroes are shown "Before" and "After" losing dozens of pounds on the advertised plan. The heroes are heroic because of the results of your business.

Again, you benefit from showcasing your customers' results because your marketing shows unbiased people endorsing you; your customer benefits because their good judgment and results are publicized, raising their value or esteem among their friends or company.

How do these approaches help your marketing efforts? In all cases, you've obtained third-party "unbiased" (and thus persuasive) customer endorsement and a customer success story at no incremental cash cost to you.

Work with Them

The only thing better than an individual hero is a set of heroes. Everyone wants to be perceived as important, and you are in a position to make them feel that way. As John Chambers, CEO of Cisco, said when asked about the company's success, "We listen to what our customers tell us they want, and then we build it."

So meet with your customers' larger management team (if a company) or friends and neighbors (if an individual), and listen to them. Solicit their input on your product direction. Show you're trying to understand their problems. Doing noisy remodeling? Invite the neighbors to an open house where you'll hear their concerns. Doing dentistry? Offer to do a lunchtime informational talk and open Q&A on nutrition, teeth, and current dentistry at your customers' company. Don't be shy—ask to come talk to their people. The worst they can say is "no"—and the best thing they can do is let you come talk to the screening committee first. Exposure is good. From an entrepreneurial marketing standpoint, even going through the process of attempting the partnership gives you exposure to an entirely new set of potential customers.

Summary: How do you increase customer retention via positive reinforcement, by offering a reward? Highlight your customers' successes.

- ▸ Provide proof of brilliance.
- ▸ Make them famous.
- ▸ Work with them.

Parting Thought: Lock-in

The best situation for customer retention is one where your product is not only safe and useful, but ideally inseparable from the customer's business.

The best situation for customer retention is one where your product is not only safe and useful, but ideally inseparable from the customer's business—where your company and product are now "locked in," considered too hard to easily remove, and purchased as much because you're available and don't require search costs as because of the value of your product.

Need an example of lock-in? Think about how often you would have liked to change a vendor or service provider—and think about how much money was then spent fixing or buying more of that product from the same vendor or provider because "it was just too hard to move."

Lock-in insulates your business from minor management or mood changes at your clients' companies, small and infrequent errors, and low-level competition. How do you get lock-in? Some possible business tactics:

- ▸ **Be available:** Integrate with their purchasing process. Become the default, easy choice for them. For example, link your web pages from their intranet. Get your number on their speed-dial system. Leave your order forms on their welcome mat or desk at work. Call them and e-mail them on a regular basis to check in and see whether they need your service.

- ▸ **Be trustworthy:** Consult with them on their business processes. You're not just an expert in one product (lawnmowing), you're their industry guide on the field of what your product does (lawn and garden care and maintenance). Be a consultant, not just a salesperson to them.

- ▸ **Be seemingly immovable:** Be impossible to remove. Be so integrated into their systems, or have your equipment installed on their premises, or have such a thorough log of their preferences and needs that the thought of trying to establish that situation with someone else intimidates them.

If you want long-term success you must be more than friendly; you must be indispensable.

Chapter 9

Avoid Common Mistakes
Make Only Uncommon Mistakes

"All great discoveries are made by mistake."

—Young's Law

"Experience is the name everyone gives to their mistakes."

—Oscar Wilde

I**F YOU WERE PERFECT, YOU'D ALREADY BE DONE. EVERY MARKETER MAKES** mistakes. But as an entrepreneur with a limited budget and only a few chances to make your business a success, the goal is to avoid making *too many* mistakes.

This chapter will provide you with brief descriptions of the top five high-risk situations and associated blunders *every* marketer has made in their career, and will give you a "three-step plan" for each situation to ensure you don't commit the same errors.

The top five traps include the following:

▶ **Betting on the big event: gambling instead of planning:** Spending all your marketing dollars in one place without calculating the odds of success first.

- ▶ **Consultant failure: knowing what not to outsource:** Inadvertently making your business' success or failure depend on your hired consultant's success or failure.

- ▶ **Product? What product?** Overmarketing without business substance to back up your claims.

- ▶ **If you can't measure it, it doesn't exist:** Completing a marketing program and realizing you have no idea if it "worked" or not, or how to improve it the next time.

- ▶ **Simple is good: sunk by excess complexity:** Making it hard for your prospective customers to understand and purchase your product.

The good news is that you don't need to learn from your mistakes. That's the expensive, painful way to learn. Instead, learn from *other people's* mistakes, as shown in the following pages, and you'll be as prepared, without the pain.

Betting on the Big Event: Gambling Instead of Planning

The first common entrepreneurial marketing error is to gamble on big events—for example, spending your entire budget on a single trade-show appearance.

The first common entrepreneurial marketing error is to gamble on big events—for example, spending your entire budget on a single trade-show appearance. Attending a trade show, sponsoring a major seminar series, or even purchasing a television advertising spot can be prohibitively expensive. If the event doesn't generate the expected associated volume of sales, you may soon have no company to market.

It is singularly appropriate that so many industry trade shows are held in Las Vegas, given the magnitude of the risks involved in such a one-shot expenditure. Consider that in the late 1990s, more than *half* of the companies exhibiting at large trade shows didn't reappear the next year.

That statistic doesn't mean you shouldn't use events—it just suggests you should be cautious, and do some planning before you commit. You don't want to be the entrepreneur walking back from Las Vegas with a single poker chip, five business cards from people who were "possibly interested in purchasing, maybe, sometime," a drained budget, and a vague sense that you would have made more money betting on the roulette wheel than on attending the trade show.

Follow the three-step approach below to *plan*, instead of *gamble*.

Ask the Numbers Questions

What are my total costs of attending this event? Remember that your booth or venue floor space only accounts for a fraction of your costs. You will typically spend at least as much as the cost of your space on power, phone, drayage and shipping, setup and teardown, travel, housing and food for you and your staff, temporary booth staff costs, and of course lost productivity (the opportunity cost of having you and your staff at the event instead of doing something else, such as making customer sales calls).

What are my total available potential leads from this event? If the event will attract 1,000 people, it could be argued that your total potential leads are those thousand. Or, you could claim that the 2,000 who registered also should be considered valid potential leads, as you'll get a list of those contacts from the show organizer for later telemarketing as well. Or, you could claim that each visitor will tell at least two friends about what they saw, so the total impact is 3,000. Alternatively, you may believe that only the attendees count, and only half are qualified buyers (versus simply curious passers-by), so the true lead number is only 500. Regardless of your methodology, you must choose a number.

What is the relative likelihood of capturing a potential sales lead? If you have a total of 1,000 potential leads, how many are you likely to capture as contacts? How many of the captured contacts are likely to mature into leads, and of those how many will turn into deals, and at what average deal size?

Once you've assessed those three numbers, you can make a rough guess at whether the event is worthwhile, with some simple math:

$$\text{profit} = [\text{\# of potential leads}] \times [\text{likelihood of making sale}]$$
$$\times [\text{size of sale}] - [\text{total costs of attending event}]$$

If your profit is sufficiently large—it should be at least 2-to-5 times your cost—do the event.

If your profit is sufficiently large—it should be at least 2-to-5 times your cost—do the event.

Equip Yourself to Be Successful

If you were standing on a street corner in a city, trying to convince passers-by to give you money, what would you do? Would you choose any random street and stand there with your hand out, or would you examine streets for kind-hearted pedestrian traffic, set out a money-collection bowl, put on a bit of a show, and leave yourself enough time at the end of the day to get to a bank?

Too many marketers seem to believe that simply being at a trade show is sufficient to generate leads and close sales. These marketers have no compelling materials or demonstration with which to lure passers-by into their booth. They have no card-scanner or even a bowl for business cards. They have no reason for prospective customers to provide their contact information—and worse, these managers have no follow-up mechanism. If, by some mischance, they obtained a large number of contacts, these managers have no way of sorting the contacts, qualifying them, parsing them out to telesales or direct-sales clients, or following up in a timely and educated manner.

If you don't have both a way to obtain contacts, and a way to correctly process the burst of potential leads, you will have doubly wasted your event opportunity. You would have been better off spending the money not on the single big event, but instead on a larger number of smaller marketing programs over the course of several weeks or months. So be prepared for success—put yourself in the customers' shoes. Why should they stop by your booth? What will they see there? What will you talk about? What will they leave with? Why should they give you a business card or scan their badge? Answer those questions first, and then go write the materials, build the demonstrations, rent the badge-scanner or business-card fishbowl, and satisfy your potential customer.

Shop Around

You should always be suspicious of events you're being pitched until their value (return on investment—ROI) is proven.

Entrepreneurial marketing and sales professionals like you are highly susceptible to good marketing and sales approaches from others. But you should always be suspicious of events you're being pitched until their value (return on investment—ROI) is proven. As Groucho Marx said, "I'd never join any country club that would have me." Many entrepreneurial marketers fail by betting on events that they've been sold, instead of *choosing* events that fit with their strategic plan, target audience, and desired ROI.

So be sure there's a fit.

▶ **Be sure the event fits your audience:** Just because an event is big doesn't mean it's a good event for you. In fact, it may not be as productive from a lead-generation standpoint if it's too big a show. FOSE is a giant government computer technology show—and therefore might *not* be appropriate for a specialty retailer of computer keyboards, or for a government-oriented aerospace company, who will be lost in the crowd and ignored by the audience, respectively. *Go where people want what you have to sell, and can find you.*

▶ **Be sure the event meets your ROI goals.** There are lots of possible events and shows you can attend or sponsor. Do you make more money per dollar you spend in costs (better ROI) from actually having a booth in the show, or a hospitality suite near the show, or a private seminar in the city a month after the show, or attending a different show entirely? If you're going to bet on the event, bet on the event with the largest estimated payoff, and bear in mind that *your* participation (booth, suite, seminar) may not have to be the *main* event to benefit from it.

In short, be a careful customer for big events. Shop around for the best situation for your business. Be conservative in your planning of profits, generous in your estimation of costs. Be pessimistic about possible outcomes, and ask if it's still worth attending the event in the "worst case" situation. If you do decide to take a risk, prepare wisely and make the most of the opportunity.

Summary: How can you avoid failure? Match event costs with expected profits.

▶ Always do the math on expected costs and resultant sales, underestimating sales.

▶ Equip yourself to make the most of the event.

▶ Shop around, and understand where your money could be best spent.

Consultant Failure: Knowing What Not to Outsource

The second common entrepreneurial marketing error is to rely too much on consultants for critical aspects of your business. There's an old joke that says "A consultant is someone who borrows your watch to tell you what time it is, then charges you for doing so. A bad consultant tells you the wrong time, and keeps your watch." Many entrepreneurs forget that if the consultant they hired fails to perform a critical task, *it's not only the consultant who fails*.

Exercise caution in hiring and using consultants or outside vendors, and follow the three-step plan to ensure you're protected from their potential failure, even as you engage them to assist in creating your success.

The second common entrepreneurial marketing error is to rely too much on consultants for critical aspects of your business.

Be Sure You're Hiring a Great Consultant

If a consultant hasn't done prior work for you, how do you know they'll deliver what you need? As when hiring a house painter, using a dry-cleaner,

147

or looking for a good automobile mechanic, you should seek out references (and not just those the consultant or vendor provides to you) and examine their prior work.

This type of "due diligence" is critical, not so much to avoid the obviously poor consultants as to ascertain "fit" with your project. The consultant may be an expert, but not in your area—or expert in your area, just not in your style. Apple Computer's advertising agency has produced brilliant campaigns appealing to the young, technologically savvy, and stylish—but would that agency be appropriate for the more conservative clothier Brooks Brothers? In short, examine and discuss with your prospective consultant what you want as a finished product, in what timeframe, in what budget, and with what process. Up-front specifics yield later satisfaction.

Do you think your consultant is "obviously" good, so you can skip the planning and reference check steps? Be careful. In late 2002, Kenneth Lonchar, CFO of the multi-billion-dollar software company Veritas, was fired for falsely claiming to have had a Stanford MBA when he was hired. Analysts downgraded the company stock because they felt his reference falsification had implications as to his ability to correctly do his job. *No business, and no level of employee hire, should warrant making reference checks optional.*

Be sure to check your consultant's references. A good consultant will not only provide references of great clients, but also clients where things didn't go as planned. Go off the list—ask the referrals to name other companies the consultant worked for that the consultant didn't name as references.

Be sure to check your consultant's references. A good consultant will not only provide references of great clients, but also clients where things didn't go as planned.

Communicate, Communicate, Communicate ... and Be Specific

Specifics, especially around payment, matter. Be clear, and be sure your clarity is codified in a written contract.

Some examples of specifics include:

- ▶ **Ownership:** Be sure that your company owns the rights to the results the consultant produces.

- ▶ **Costs:** Be sure costs are segmented, capped, and keyed to deliverables. If a consultant promises an ad design with two reviews for $1,000 assuming five hours of work, and it takes them ten hours of work, you shouldn't owe additional funds or get a half-done design.

- ▶ **Timelines:** Be sure deadlines are clearly established, rational, and set to dates far before you actually need the results. Be wary of a consultant who proposes or agrees to unreasonable deadlines; they either don't know what they're doing or aren't being honest with you.

▶ **Deliverables:** Be sure deliverables are results-oriented, measurable, non-subjective, and independent of spend or tactics. For example, if a consultant promises that a direct-mail campaign will garner 100 calls, they should be willing to send out more than the agreed-on number of mail pieces. You need the lead result (the calls)—you don't care about the mechanism (number of mail pieces).

Of course, payment should always be based on timely results, with significant penalties if time or results are missed.

Have a Backup Plan

The last thing you can do to avoid failure is to have a backup plan. Even if you've worked with the consultant many times before and are happy with their work, statistically speaking it is certain that eventually something won't happen as planned. It may be due to environmental factors, such as a snowstorm delaying a shipment, or it may be due to human error—but either way, if you don't have a backup plan, your business will suffer the consequences.

Backup plans don't need to be complex or massive in nature, and should be scaled in proportion to the criticality of the deliverable from the consultant. Items of low criticality deserve smaller plans. For example, the creation of the sign for the podium at your seminar doesn't require a large backup plan, as your backup plan if your consultant fails to create a nice sign is "don't have a podium sign." Conversely, issues like "keynote speaker gets sick/fails to show" deserve larger backup plans, such as paying a second analyst or having a second executive "on tap" as a speaker.

Write down the plan with the same dependencies and implementation diligence applied as to your primary plan (someone needs to schedule the backup speaker as well as the primary)—then be sure different parties are responsible for the backup plan, to avoid single points of failure and to lower risk (you don't want the same room scheduler responsible for booking your primary room and double-checking a few days in advance to be sure it's booked, for example). Then, establish a cut-over date or sequence of events to move to backup plans in an orderly fashion—for example, if you don't have the primary speaker at the event by one hour prior to their speaking slot, the secondary speaker starts warming up. Like any disaster preparedness system, the system works best when well planned, redundant, and proactively engaged rather than invoked at the last minute out of necessity.

*B*ackup plans don't need to be complex or massive in nature, and should be scaled in proportion to the criticality of the deliverable from the consultant.

149

In short, trust no one. Even consultants are human, and make mistakes. As you will as well. But as the entrepreneur, you're the most closely involved in your venture's success. So plan accordingly.

Summary: How can you avoid failure? Keep the critical things under your control.

- ▶ Check references.
- ▶ Communicate and align expectations.
- ▶ Have a backup plan.

Product? What Product?

The third common entrepreneurial marketing error is to over-promise and under-deliver on your product or service. You know what this is like as a customer—you've had the experience of unwrapping your latest purchase and having that sinking feeling in your stomach as you think "this isn't what I thought I bought," or "it sounded so much better when they described it to me." As a customer, in the future you'd probably avoid the vendor from whom you made the purchase. As a vendor, you don't want your customers feeling this way. So follow the three-step plan to avoid over-promising and under-delivering.

The third common entrepreneurial marketing error is to over-promise and under-deliver on your product or service.

Understand Your Customers

Key to success is *matching customer expectations and product delivery*. In every market there will be customers for products with different attributes. For example, 99-cent stores serve a different set of purchasing needs and customers than does Nordstrom—and those 99-cent stores would fail at marketing and sales lead generation if they focused their efforts on attracting purchasers seeking the Nordstrom levels of service and quality.

So do you know your customers? What's the thing they buy the most from you? What's the average amount of money they spend per purchase with you? Have you surveyed your customers lately (directly, via mail, or online) on what they'd most like to see you continue, start, and stop doing? You may be surprised to find that you think you're a 99-cent store, but you're satisfying customers who care about Nordstrom service levels ... or vice versa.

Sell What You Have, in a Way that Appeals to Your Customers—By Matching Features to Needs

Only once you understand your customers' needs can you speak to those needs in the right way.

For example, two competing sport-utility vehicle companies launched essentially similar products in the same timeframe. One, proud of the technical engine advances they had achieved, touted their fuel economy. The other, recognizing that the current purchasers were more family oriented, emphasized the safety of their vehicle. The safety message won. Those marketers were listening to their customers, not to their own egos.

Notably, neither of the actual vehicles were substantially different from each other—they had comparable engines and safety features. The difference in marketing was purely one of emphasis, or spin. *If you present your business with the correct message to the correct customers, they'll buy.* You don't need to sell more features if they don't care about those features. If you have a 99-cent video store and you've correctly found a 99-cent audience, you'll do fine telling them about how much money they'll save instead of telling them about your great quality.

Resist Temptation:
Talk Selectively about Futures, from a Preplanned Presentation or Set of Notes—Never Let Yourself Be Caught in an Impromptu Discussion of Specific Future Plans

If you're enthusiastic about your business, it's easy to wax poetic about your vision. Your challenge is that customers don't want to wait. *What you tell them will change their behavior.* So be careful.

▶ **Do talk about futures to explain your current product or service features.** Does your product have features for future use? Examples include tractors with power takeoff units, digital video cameras with Firewire ports, and tax preparation service with "free audit protection." Flexibility is worth money to some customers—there may be people willing to pay more for these products, *even before the additive technology* (the things that take advantage of those extra ports and connections) *exists*. Selling futures is important when selling an extensible product, in that it augments the value of the current product.

▶ **Do talk about futures to deliberately slow down the customer's purchase.** If your competitor has a significant technical lead, but you have larger cash

151

reserves, you may announce a vision of a product that's hugely more compelling than their current offering to deliberately stall the purchasing process and give your company an opportunity to build a superior product while the customer waits. But bear in mind that this type of pre-announcement starts a timer, counting down to the point where the customer loses patience and makes a purchase of what's currently available. As you race to build product, your competitors will scramble to counter the move you've just pre-announced. If you stall the customer correctly and deliver your product as they decide to make a purchase, you win. If, on the other hand, your competitor moved farther than you during the delay, or if you missed delivering before the customer made a choice, the market will move on without you, and bury you in the process.

▶ **Don't sell nonexistent specifics.** Specifics make a product a promise to a customer instead of a vision. Vision is "Our stereo should work with future headphones." Specifics are "Our stereo will have a connector that makes it work with the HC128 headphones for at least five years." Don't build a specific product release ("the next version") over a glass of wine with a customer. Don't promise dates or release numbers or features unless they are in the context of a signed contract with engineering fees that are already in line with your company's strategic objectives—and don't ever make a deal for a current product contingent on a not-yet-imagined future feature.

Don't ever make a deal for a current product contingent on a not-yet-imagined future feature.

In short, be careful balancing present business reality against your vision for your business. It may sometimes be necessary to "sell the sizzle, not the steak"—to communicate the product benefits rather than features or applications—but there is a fine line between explaining *current* value by communicating vision and strategic direction, and outright sales of nonexistent *future* product. Don't tape-record the sizzle—sell it only when it's coming from an actual steak on the grill.

Summary: How can you avoid failure? Sell the benefits of what you have.

▶ Understand your customers, and what they value about your business.

▶ Sell what you have, not what you're planning to have—presented so your customers can understand how what you have today matches what they value.

▶ Use "vision" presentations carefully, in a pre-thought-out way, to stall competition or explain why owning the *current* product is of *more* value than waiting.

If You Can't Measure It, It Doesn't Exist

The fourth common entrepreneurial marketing error is to neglect to measure results. A recent report by the CMO Council didn't mince words on this topic: "The typical Chief Marketing Officer ... is able to neither measure nor systematically communicate on the fundamental business processes in the marketing function and their results. This can set the stage for a CMO's failure."

It's not hard to understand why lack of measurement would lead to failure. Would *you* give a large bank check to an advertising agency that couldn't prove to you that they'd increased your business? It's difficult to justify additional marketing spend—much less use the feedback to improve and optimize marketing programs—when the impact of the current programs isn't clearly measured or understood.

There's little excuse for lack of measurement. Measurement can be quite straightforward when included as an element of marketing program design. Like building a house, it's relatively simple to add wiring during construction—but becomes significantly harder after the whole structure is completed. Many managers forget to build in the necessary features in the beginning, and consequently fail in the end. So start early in your planning, and follow the three-step plan to ensure you have the right results.

Understand What You Want to Measure—Revenue

Overall, your marketing programs are about *making money for you*. But do you know which programs are best? For example, if you sent direct mail to 500 people for $50, and then 5,000 people for only $100, is the latter situation a better program?

The answer is that you don't know. The measurement isn't relevant—as what you care about is not cost per mail, but cost per *sale*, or at least cost per qualified lead (or at a minimum, cost per response). You could have sent mail to 5,000 chimpanzees, and no matter what the cost, it would likely have not generated more sales than your mail to 500 cash-bearing humans.

What you'd like to know is how many people who became aware of you through your program went on to eventually buy something (versus the number of people who became aware of you through other more or less expensive methods). *Always tie your measurements to revenue (sales).*

The typical Chief Marketing Officer ... is able to neither measure nor systematically communicate on the fundamental business processes in the marketing function and their results. This can set the stage for a CMO's failure.

Build Ways of Measuring What You Want to Measure into Your Program

Understand the goal of your specific program, and what measurements would be meaningful. For example, if the goal of a program is awareness, do you measure the number of mail pieces sent, or the phone calls you receive in response to those pieces? If the goal of the program is contact capture, do you measure clicks to your web page, or completed registration forms?

Figure out how you'll associate a program with a result. For example, if you're using a web banner, can you automatically count clicks or views of the banner? Or must you rely on a phone question when the respondents call in, or multiple-choice checkbox option on a reply postcard, asking "how did you hear about us?"

Assess whether there's sufficient incentive for prospective customers to assist you in measuring. For example, do customers receive a gift or rebate for telling you where they heard about you? Can you automatically track where they heard about you based on color of returned postcard, or code embedded in the web link, so that no explicit incentive is needed? Does your product require regular service, and can it automatically report on its use during that period (for example, the "black box" in some cars and airplanes)?

Be sure you can maintain direct program association to sale, or even multiple program association. For example, if you associate a program with a contact—John Doe attended a presentation on January 1, 2010—when John's company purchases your product, can you generate a report showing all the marketing events by date that touched John and his fellow staff?

As you build your programs, remember to think about how to capture and tag the contact information as belonging to a certain marketing program, and how this data will remain associated with the lead through the course of the sale.

Once You Have Data, Don't Change Too Many Things about Your Program at Once

You can't measure the effect of a single change if you're simultaneously making multiple changes.

Many managers fail by lack of measurement through errors of attribution—they spend money on the wrong thing because they believe prior measurement identified that thing as the source of their success.

What's an error of attribution? In the movie *All of Me* starring Steve Martin, a leading character happens to flush a toilet at the same time that a phone rings. He continues to flush several times, coincident with the ring, and then is puzzled when he flushes and the phone does not ring. He's making an error of attribution, incorrectly associating his action with coincidental events that don't actually have a cause-and-effect relationship.

To use a marketing example, if you did a bulk mailing that was successful, and compared it to a bulk mailing that was less successful but occurred at a different time, sent to a different group of people, using a different message, you'd be unable to determine what made the latter mailing more successful than the former.

To remedy the situation, you could have split a bulk mailing into two groups, both to the same audience, with the same designs and titles, but one different variable—for example, one different title or offer. At the end of the mailing you'd be able to make some definitive statements about the value of the different messages or offers.

In short, move deliberately. Doing smaller, more focused marketing programs where you can understand the results is far more valuable than gambling on one big event, then changing *everything* and gambling again if your first attempt didn't work.

Summary: How can you avoid failure? Measure sales, and build in measurement methods.

- ▶ Understand what to measure—and always measure the program's linkage to sales.

- ▶ Build ways of measuring into your marketing program.

- ▶ Change one variable—one aspect of your program—at a time, then repeat and re-measure.

Simple Equals Good: Sunk by Excess Complexity

The fifth common entrepreneurial marketing error is to engage in excess complexity. Most people can only hold five to nine pieces of information in their short-term memory at one time. If you present a marketing message longer than that, people won't remember it. It's not surprising that some of the most successful companies in the world have the shortest slogans and messages—for example, consider Sony Corporation's "It's a Sony!" tagline.

Yet marketers have been known to insist on hyper-complex response mechanisms, multi-page surveys and registration forms, and cryptic calls to

Doing smaller, more focused marketing programs where you can understand the results is far more valuable than gambling on one big event, then changing everything and gambling again if your first attempt didn't work.

155

action, even as they try to attract more leads.

When selling or generating leads, your goal should be to make the process as frictionless as possible for the buyer, as every barrier you put in their way is one more opportunity for them to change their mind about buying. So think like a customer (or ask your colleagues to do so), and follow the three-step plan to ensure you're protected from their potential failure while using them for success.

Say It Simply

Words can create barriers to purchase. Your potential customers have a limited attention span. If they need to think at all, much less use a dictionary to decipher the materials that are supposedly selling them on the product, they won't buy what you have to sell.

For example, a product that "leverages inherent efficiencies in operations slack-time" is less attractive to prospective customers than one that does the same thing by "using spare time." Products that "consumers agree produce an enhanced flavor sensation" are less immediately appealing than products that "people think taste better," and a "solution for business continuity" gets less attention than one that talks about "zero failures."

Similarly, drug and tobacco companies often put their marketing messages in large, easy-to-read print, while relegating their federally mandated warnings to small, gray typeface containing multiple four-syllable words at the end of the page. After all, who wouldn't want to "Go where the flavor is," while many of us would likely want to skip side effects which include seratonergic syndrome, cogitation issues, or gastrointestinal issues!

Good marketing messages should be thought of as haiku—they make a complex statement in a minimum number of easily understood words. Thought of in four sections, like haiku, any marketing should achieve the following:

▶ Catch the prospective customers' attention, and state your product or company's value in the title.

▶ Repeat the value, slightly elaborated, in the first section.

▶ Deliver a concise summary of who your company is, what you do, and how you address the need and create the value that you previously talked about, in the second section.

▶ End with directions on learning more (web link, phone number) and a *single* call to action ("call now to take a test drive," or "get a whitepaper on cost savings by faxing us now").

If customers need to think at all, much less use a dictionary to decipher the materials that are supposedly selling them on the product, they won't buy what you have to sell.

If elegantly constructed, like a great haiku, your message will be shorter than the paragraphs above, and yet evoke a sense of the value you convey, stay in your customers' minds, and persuade them that they need to know more.

Make It Simple to Do

Customers are lazy. Why should they exert extra effort to help you? After all, they're paying *you* money. So as the grade-school advice says, KISS—Keep It Simple, Stupid.

▶ **Promotions and rebates:** How many steps does it take your customer to get their rebate? Have you tried it yourself, as customer "John Doe"? If your customer has to complete 15 steps over the course of hours or days, including tasks such as obtaining copies of their purchasing department's invoice, circling and highlighting numbers, and mailing in a certain size envelope to a certain one-time address, all for a minimal reward, they probably won't bother. Don't force your customers to jump through too many hoops.

▶ **Product trial:** If your customer must wait more than 24 hours to obtain a response to their request for a product trial (or more than a few minutes if the trial is of an electronically available product), they're waiting too long. Even traditional bookstores and music stores are making music samples and book previews available electronically—and more than one automobile manufacturer lets you design and preview the look of your car on the Internet. Credit checks can be performed in minutes over the Internet, and many companies now make the product available if customers submit a credit card as a deposit—the product is shipped via next-day air. So don't give potential customers time to reconsider and shop elsewhere. *Respond fast.*

Don't give potential customers time to reconsider and shop elsewhere. Respond fast.

▶ **Product information and sales contact:** If your phone voicemail has menus at all, you're already sinning. If the voicemail menus have more than three options, you're in trouble, and if there's no way to speak to a human at all without a wait of longer than 30 seconds, you're a hopeless case. Be sure your product information and sales query forms are available (even if behind a registration process) via phone, response fax, and Internet—and have a live human with a real name who is reachable again available to reply to queries, even if the answer is simply "we'll need to call you back in a week."

In short, if your customer has to spend more time and attention on completing your process than they'll see in return (use $100 per hour as a value of return), you're doing them and yourself a disservice.

Don't Ask Too Much of Your Customers

Which would you rather have, 20 sets of contact information of which 10 turn out to be unqualified, or one qualified set of information? Too many entrepreneurial marketers, burned by spending too much time pursuing "junk" leads, strive to over-qualify their leads before trying to make a sale. But in their attempts to better their lead quality, they may be artificially restricting their lead flow.

Even if you have a simple process ("fill in this form, get a trial"), you may be demanding too much information, depending on the product in question and length of the form. For example, some high-end automobile dealers will let you take a test drive only after they perform a credit check, photocopy your license, and place a deposit on your credit card. But the high-end clientele these dealers are striving to attract are exactly the audience that will resent the delay, intrusion on their privacy, and "criminal background check" treatment.

Similarly, excessive demands may alter the validity of your information. A questionnaire for a free copy of *Infoworld* magazine used to ask over 50 questions, all of which required answers—and few of which allowed the user to choose "other" as an option. As a result, many participants either abandoned the survey, or filled in nonsensical answers, skewing the data. *Infoworld* now asks only seven questions, and has seen response rates rise accordingly.

Make life easy for your potential customers. Remove as much friction from the purchase process as possible for them.

Balance the value of that which you're offering against the possibility of collecting multiple bits of information over a longer set of interactions—and don't attempt to force the qualification process so that only the truly desperate reach your salespeople. Before you ask your audience even your first question, they're all equal—so don't let your questioning process drive away the good ones.

In short, make life easy for your potential customers. Remove as much friction from the purchase process as possible for them. Still don't understand this at a visceral level? Visit a local McDonald's restaurant—you can point to the beautifully photographed pictures of the food and have it given to you with no questions asked. It's the ultimate in simple product representation and frictionless commerce.

Summary: How can you avoid failure? Keep it simple for your customer.

▶ **Say it simply:** Use concise, basic descriptions.

▶ **Make it simple to do:** It should be easy to do business with you.

▶ **Don't ask too much of your customers:** All you *really* want is their business.

Parting Thought: Make Uncommon Mistakes

You now have a three-step plan to guide you through each of the five most common traps marketers experience. So are you safe? Absolutely not! You'll certainly make other mistakes as you grow your business. If you don't, you're not being aggressive and creative enough with your marketing.

But don't worry. The unwritten "fourth step" in every three-step plan is the age-old lemon lesson: when life hands you lemons, make lemonade.

Consider the number of great discoveries that were made by mistake—penicillin, Post-It brand notes, and Coca-Cola all originated because of an error. As the entrepreneur, the final outcome of any situation often rests in your hands. So when it all seems to be going wrong, relax; take a deep breath, ask what the situation lets you provide to customers, and dive in.

Appendix A

Put It All Together

"Strategy is for amateurs. Logistics is for professionals."

—Gen. Norman Schwartzkopf

AS ANYONE WHO'S EVER PUT TOGETHER A PUZZLE KNOWS, THERE'S A world of difference between having all the pieces and being able to put them together into a cohesive whole. A whole, integrated marketing program will have an effect that is larger than the sum of its parts—and understanding the whole system can be challenging even to experienced marketers. As is the case when doing a puzzle, it helps to have a picture of the completed project in front of you as an example of what you're seeking to build.

To that end, this appendix will present two examples of integrated, whole entrepreneurial marketing plans, so that you can see "the big picture" and model your plans accordingly.

Examples include:

▶ A *product-based business's marketing program*, such as would be used by a camera store or software company

▶ A *service business's marketing program*, such as would be used by a law firm or consultant

161

Like hunting and farming, it's nice to get a prospect you've chased as a new customer—but it's keeping them a customer in the long term that pays.

Marketing Programs Plan: SmallProductCo

If your business is product-based—if you're either an independent store or member of a larger company (or franchise) that sells things you can put in boxes, such as cameras, books, computer software, antiques, arts and crafts, or the like—then this marketing programs plan is for you. SmallProductCo is represented as a T-shirt store, but the general form of its marketing plan and tactics could be adapted to any products business.

Context: SmallProductCo is a (hypothetical) store in Boston, MA that sells T-shirts featuring both original designs by the owner and licensed designs from major suppliers (such as Disney). The owner of SmallProductCo (SPC) would like to increase sales over the next three months.

Situation Analysis and Conclusions

SPC took a few days and put together their initial marketing plan analysis. While they were helped by the fact that they'd kept diligent sales records in a spreadsheet, much of the data for their analyses came from talking with their business counterparts and chatting with their customers (an informal checklist survey was done by the checkout clerks). SPC did *not* spend thousands of dollars and months of work on their plan—and while they ended up with less data than they would have if they'd engaged a professional market research firm, the data they had was (they believed) enough to build a quick plan.

3 C/4 P Analysis

SPC started by building a 3 C/4 P matrix and studying their current market landscape (Figure A-1).

While initially it had appeared that there were only two groups of sellers, independent and corporate, and groups were otherwise the same, the analysis did contain some surprises.

▶ T's & Things had been worrying SPC because of their low price—but it looked like they were really in the business of providing plain white shirts in bulk to department stores. While it looked like a profitable business, SPC didn't feel that they could beat T's & Things' prices at this time.

162

Product						
Company	**Colored Shirts?**	**Disney Designs?**	**University Designs?**	**Different Weights?**	**Different Styles?**	**Interstate Delivery**
Small Product Co	✗	✗		✗	✗	✗
Mr. T-Shirt				✗		
T-Shirts R Us	✗			✗		
Big T & Sons				✗		
T's & Things				✗		
Harvard Bookstore	✗	✗	Some		✗	✗
Macy's	✗	✗				✗
Nordstrom's (Teen Store)	✗	✗			✗	✗

Price				
	Avg Per Shirt	**Avg # Per Deal**	**Volume Discounts?**	**Takes Credit Card**
Small Product Co	$10	3	✗	✗
Mr. T-Shirt	$9	1		✗
T-Shirts R Us	$14	1		✗
Big T & Sons	$12	2		✗
T's & Things	$5	10	✗	
Harvard Bookstore	$17	1	✗	✗
Macy's	$25	1		✗
Nordstrom's (Teen Store)	$35	1		✗

Promotion				
	Coupons	**News Ads**	**Yellow Pages**	**Posters**	**Web Site**
Small Product Co			✗		✗
Mr. T-Shirt			✗	✗	✗
T-Shirts R Us			✗		✗
Big T & Sons		✗	✗	✗	✗
T's & Things			✗		
Harvard Bookstore					✗
Macy's	✗				✗
Nordstrom's (Teen Store)	✗				✗

Figure A-1. 3-C/4-P analysis (continued on next page)

Placement				
Company	**Web Site**	**Storefront**	**College Bookstore**	**Macy's**
Small Product Co		✗		
Mr. T-Shirt	✗	✗		
T-Shirts R Us		✗		
Big T & Sons	✗	✗		
T's & Things				
Harvard Bookstore	✗	✗	✗	
Macy's	✗	✗		✗
Nordstrom's (Teen Store)	✗	✗		

Company							
	Annual Sales	**# Emp's**	**Annual Growth**	**# Shops**	**Partners**	**Reputation**	**Years in Shirt Biz**
Small Product Co	$1mm	3	10%	1		5-star	10
Mr. T-Shirt	$500K	2	20%	1	1	2-star	8
T-Shirts R Us	$1mm	1	20%	1		4-star	4
Big T & Sons	$250K	4	20%	1		3-star	8
T's & Things	$500k	5	20%	1		2-star	6
Harvard Bookstore	$7mm	100	3%	3	3	4-star	20
Macy's	$35mm	1000's	5%	100's	4	3-star	3
Nordstrom's (Teen Store)	$27mm	1000's	5%	100's	5	2-star	8

Customers			
	Avg # Shirts/ Deal	**Frequency of Buys**	**Other Places Shopped**	**Type Shirt**
Small Product Co	3	3	T's & Things	
Mr. T-Shirt	2	2	T's & Things	
T-Shirts R Us	1	1	T's & Things	
Big T & Sons	$250K	3	T-Shirts R Us	
T's & Things	$500k	4	T-Shirts R Us	
Harvard Bookstore	$7mm	5	T-Shirts R Us	
Macy's	$35mm	3	T-Shirts R Us	
Nordstrom's (Teen Store)	$27mm	9	T's & Things	

Figure A-1. 3-C/4-P analysis (continued)

- ▶ SPC was doing far less advertising and promotion than the other stores.
- ▶ Only Harvard was offering university designs (and those only from Harvard), despite the large number of universities in the area.
- ▶ SPC's customers were college-aged, similar to those of Macy's and the big chains, but different from the other stores, who catered more to high-school or adults. When surveyed, SPC's customers cited the original designs available at SPC.

SWOT Analysis

The subsequent SWOT analysis was taken from the initial 3 C/4 P analysis.

Strengths	Weaknesses
• Unique designs • Proven appeal to college age • Existing licensing relationship	• Minimal national recognition • Small/weak corp. bargaining position • Semi-seasonal wear
Opportunities	**Threats**
• Not doing any promotion currently • No other university licensees • No other designs resold through corp.	• Corp. relationship adds time/focus risk • Designers are cheap, can be bought • Low-cost competitor has corp. partners

Figure A-2. SWOT analysis

What the SWOT analysis suggested was that two routes to increase sales were possible. In the short term, simply adding some local promotional tactics to match the visibility of other shops should drive additional sales—though such a tactic ran the risk of disturbing the delicate balance SPC had achieved with its competitors, and SPC couldn't afford a price war. The second, longer-term approach would be for SPC to partner with some larger entities, thus increasing volume and awareness. If such a partnership included licensing university logos, SPC could also partially avoid the seasonal effect (large chains tended to carry fewer general T-shirts in the non-summer months, but stocked university logowear year-round). If such a corporate relationship happened, SPC also considered expanding its line of T-shirt designs intended to be worn as nightshirts, again keeping it in the stores year-round. An expanded Internet presence was also an option, depending on the out-of-state publicity SPC could obtain as an exclusive licensor of university logos (with associated links from the school sites).

Customer Purchase Process

Finally, an analysis of the customer purchase process revealed that SPC's "sales funnel" was remarkably frictionless—in fact, far too frictionless. Of the customers who found their way to SPC's store, a very high percentage (almost 8 of every 10 visitors) purchased at least one shirt. To the owners of SPC, this meant that to raise sales, they couldn't just do a better job of serving their existing visitors (a process that would have involved simply asking those who didn't buy "why not," and adjusting their products or presentation thereof accordingly). Instead, SPC would need to raise the total volume of visitors to the shop—raising awareness of SPC.

Marketing Program(s) Objective

Every marketing program should have a specific objective: Why are you doing these programs (versus other programs)? The objective should refer to situation analysis and customer purchase process—Is the aim to "increase awareness" or "move to purchase"?

Quantity versus Quality

As the initial customer purchase process analysis had shown that SPC wasn't losing customers who'd made it to their store, and the price of their shirts wasn't that high, SPC assumed that their goal would be one of quantity of prospective customers. (If their products had been more expensive, or the average deal size much lower than that of their competitors, or customers who made it to the store were leaving due to a mismatch between their expectations and the type of goods being sold, the goal might have been one of quantity.)

Choosing Goals

SPC was currently making about $500,000 per year in sales. They felt it would not be unreasonable to attempt a 20 percent increase in sales over the next three months—for an increase in yearly revenues of $100,000 (20 percent of $500,000).

Since three months was a quarter of a year, they'd need to see revenues of one-quarter of $100,000, or about $25,000 in additional sales.

SPC's average deal size was $30 (three T-shirts at $10 each), so they'd need to achieve an additional 833 deals, or about 64 more deals per week. (Alternatively, they could try to increase the average deal size to more shirts.)

Since 8 of every 10 people entering the store made a purchase, SPC assumed they'd need to get 833 times (10/8) additional people, (1,042 people) into their storefront. Note that this estimate was probably too low, as it's likely that as they reach out to more people who are less familiar with SPC, the conversion rate of browsers to buyers will be less than 8 of every 10.

Based on the number of people who agreed to fill out their survey, as well as data SPC obtained from their contacts at the larger department stores, the results of a newspaper ad they'd run last year advertising a sale, and Internet statistics on likely response rate, SPC assumed that only 10 of every 100 people they could get mailing addresses for would show up at their shop—so they needed at least 8,330 contact addresses.

Lastly, SPC knew from reading the advertising guarantees of their local newspapers and local tourist web sites that they should expect no more than 0.1 percent (1 of every 1,000 people) exposed to their advertising to provide a contact address (via click through on a web banner, telephone call, or visit in response to the newspaper ad). So they needed to create about 8,330,000 "impressions" with their ads—or figure out a more effective awareness mechanism.

Tracking and Measuring

Since SPC had done very little awareness generation to date, they knew it would be critical to understand which activities worked and which didn't. They invested in three basic tracking mechanisms.

First, for less than $100, they purchased a new phone number with multi-extension capability. When people dialed the new, memorable number (1-800-shirt-me), they heard a greeting asking them to enter their extension or wait to leave a message on the general mailbox. All extensions actually rang through to the store, but SPC could examine the phone records later to understand who called extension 123 (the number listed on their postcards) and who called extension 567 (the number listed on their bumper stickers).

Second, SPC altered their web site (by using a free log analysis tool from the Internet, and hiring a local college IT student) so that they could see who came from which referring web sites, and who proceeded to buy.

Finally, SPC asked their counter staff to ask every person who came to the store "how did you hear about us?" and check off the appropriate boxes on a survey form near the register (person's name and address optional, but they were entered in a drawing for free T-shirts if they provided the infomation). If the person then bought anything, the dollar amount and items were also noted.

By implementing these three techniques, SPC felt that they'd have a much more detailed sense of which awareness techniques drove purchasers to their store.

Key Elements

Reflecting on their situation, SPC realized that they should focus on their two primary strengths: their unique designs and primarily student-type purchasers.

SPC planned to take a two-pronged approach. They would go to the universities themselves for licensing and distribution, and the universities' student organizations for primary awareness. Their plan included the following:

Friends and Family

▶ **Charity e-mail:** SPC sent an e-mail to their (and their employees') families, as well as the few hundred customer e-mails they had, explaining that in support of SPC's original designs, they'd be sponsoring a young artists competition for new designs—the winner of which would receive a substantial cash prize. E-mail recipients could help by passing on the email, and by buying a T-shirt from SPC online between certain dates, where a percent of the shirt purchase would go toward the artists' competition.

▶ **Referral program:** As an added bonus, SPC would be awarding a free shirt-per-month to the top 10 people who referred the most purchasers on the web site (the purchase form included a "referred by" field, into which purchasers were encouraged to enter the e-mail address of the person who referred them.

Community Efforts

▶ **Discussion group:** SPC started a "featured local design" area on their web site, with an associated discussion group. The designs of selected artists (submitted via web form) whom the SPC staff particularly liked were posted and feedback/discussion could be left. (The SPC team started their own blog, where each on-duty employee could post their impressions). Particularly popular designs were purchased by SPC for reproduction into T-shirts.

▶ **Affinity group:** Additionally, SPC contacted local university design classes, and notified them of the online forum and monthly "design night," where SPC would host a different local design professor speaking and provide free pizza for local students. SPC was able to leverage their "just off campus" status and appeal to this group of purchasers. SPC also planned to broadcast the speaker (and record them for web playback) via Webinar.

▶ **Extended online community:** Finally, SPC surveyed the students for their favorite bloggers—and contacted the bloggers, both inviting them to speak at the SPC design nights, and asking whether sponsorship of their blogs (by enabling the bloggers to offer custom T-shirts, for example) would be possible.

Awareness Programs

▶ **Print advertising, postering, and signage:** SPC took out advertisements in the local college papers, as well as paying for periodic postering of local college bulletin boards. SPC increased their "signage" levels by giving away large vinyl stickers featuring their logo and contact information around individual T-shirt designs. These stickers were added to every purchase package, as well as being freely available at the store and at all events SPC attended. SPC also ordered bright yellow bags with red block printing advertising SPC's web address and phone, so that all customers would become walking advertisements.

▶ **Directories:** A full-page advertisement for SPC's storefront and web site was placed in the college phone directory, offering a 10 percent discount for students presenting an ID. An ad was also placed in a "buyer's phone directory" used by stock buyers for larger chains like Macy's. (The buyer's ad made note of SPC's existing licensing agreement with Disney, awards for original designs, and made veiled references to their ability to supply university logowear.)

▶ **Online advertising and search presence:** Banner ads were placed with the top web sites associated with the local colleges, and a "Shirt-Me" graphic was developed for distribution to individuals' sites. (People referring more than a certain number of visitors or purchasers to SPC got a free T-shirt.) By seeding a sufficient number of Shirt-Me graphic web links, SPC assumed that they would also start appearing in the local web search listings—but to be sure, they spent a limited amount of money to appear in local listings for "college T-shirts" and "art shirts."

▶ **Direct mail/e-mail:** While telemarketing was not used (the costs to do telemarketing versus the amount of increased sales likely to be generated didn't seem to make telemarketing worthwhile), two contact lists were rented: a list of attendees at a local college art festival, and the list of all university nonsports groups. The first list was sent an invitation to the web site and "design night" series; the second list was sent the "free shirts for your group with ads on the back" limited sponsorship offer. (SPC wanted to be selective in their shirt sponsorship and avoid the sports teams, believing that the typical sports viewers were not their target market for "original art design" shirts.) SPC considered a full catalog, but decided to start with a simple postcard featuring color photos of two to three top-selling shirts. If the web site and postcards generated enough interest to justify risking the costs of a catalog later, they would consider producing one.

▶ **Live event presence:** SPC researched the upcoming college-area street fairs, and arranged to have a booth at each event, where they distributed information on "design night," registered people for the SPC electronic newsletter, sold shirts and handed out SPC stickers. Additionally, SPC contacted the local community center and offered to present an evening lecture on "making your art commercially successful as clothing," wherein they'd describe the process of transferring art to T-shirts for later sale.

▶ **News:** During the process of taking out advertising in the college papers, SPC contacted the social calendar editors and notified them of the "design night" series. SPC offered to allow any reporters access to the speakers at a private pre-night dinner, and provided a press release about the series to all the newspapers.

▶ **Availability:** SPC added to its web site by opening an "Ebay Store" and "Yahoo Store"—both of which handled the complexities of online credit card payments, fraud, chargebacks, and so forth for a fee. SPC hired a local high school student part-time to post electronic images of their shirts, answer customer e-mail, and pack shirts for shipping.

Direct Partnering

▶ SPC is negotiating with the local colleges and universities to produce T-shirts featuring university logos, in exchange for a licensing fee. SPC was able to show the offices how many current students and tourists already visited SPC's shop.

▶ SPC offered to showcase the universities' art students' work, and pay them, by sponsoring a local competition and producing a select number of shirts with the winners' designs. The universities would in exchange feature SPC's shirts in their bookstores, or at least offer signs pointing to SPC as a place to obtain the students' works.

▶ SPC offered to sponsor a limited number of university groups, by application only, where SPC would provide free shirts in exchange for SPC's logo and sponsorship note on the rear of the shirt. (SPC had calculated that the cost per shirt was $5, while each shirt would be seen by at least 500 people, making their cost per impression a quite reasonable $0.01.)

▶ Finally, SPC contacted student groups with discount offers.

Plan Overview

Combined, the elements of SPC's plan all fit on a single page, as shown in Figures A-3 and A-4.

Dependencies

When SPC reviewed their tasks, they realized that there were a few critical projects that needed to be completed before they could launch the remainder of their activities—which could then be launched in any order.

▶ Their infrastructure—phone extensions, web site tracking, and clipboard for front-register tracking—had to be in place first, as all printed materials would point people to those points of contact.

▶ Their web site blog and "featured artists" area had to be created, with artists posted, so that when people came to SPC's site in response to the awareness-generation activities they were met with content and a way to submit their own.

▶ Their first month of "design nights" had to be scheduled, with speakers (and backup speakers) confirmed, before they could start inviting the local art classes.

▶ Their presence at the street fairs had to be confirmed as soon as possi-

171

Generate Awareness	Capture Contacts	Recapture	Qualify, Sell, and Keep
• Friends (Charity) E-mail • University Design Classes • Bloggers • College Newspapers • Community and College Bulletin Boards (Flyers) • College Phonebook • Buyers Phonebook • Banner Ads • E-mail – Purchased Lists	*Web* • How heard about us (auto: unique URL accessed?) • "Account" for multiple purchases • Contact info, indexed by e-mail or phone no. • Featured local designs with discussion group • Company Blog *Phone* • How heard about us (auto: phone extension/no. dialed) • In-person responses (below) *In Person–Store* • How heard about us • Contact info • Amount bought ($) • Came in by phone or live *In Person–Events* • How heard about us • Contact info • Amount bought (at fairs) • Webcase (design night)	*Several lists* • Web accounts • Web discussion group • Phoned in • Came to store • Came to design night • Live • Via Webinar	See Offer Table for next offers extended ...

Figure A-3. Example offer table

ble, as every ad they placed in local papers would ideally say "come see us at [the fairs]" as well as listing their store front.

▶ Finally, if they chose to pursue the large buyer alliances with Macy's or similar chains, they knew it would be helpful to have the licensing arrangements completed with the universities (and SPC knew it would be helpful to have the enthusiastic references from the art classes as to their close relationship when applying to license the university logos).

	Pruchased in Last 6 Months					
Did Activity in Last 6 Months	**No Purchase EVER**	**No Purchases 6 Mos.**	**Fewer than 3 Shirts**	**3-7 Shirts**	**8-25 Shirts**	**26 or More Shirts**
Came to store 1-2 times	Gave Sticker and Design Night invite	Gave Sticker and Design Night invite	Offer "Frequent Buyer" card	Offer "Frequent Buyer" card	Offer "Group Discount" discussion	Offer "Group Discount" discussion
Came to store 3-5 times	Gave Sticker and Design Night invite	Survey/Interview why not buy lately				
Came to store 6+ times	Survey/Interview why not buy					
Visited web site, bought						
Visited web site, joined forum						
Called store 1-2 times						
Called store 3-5 times						
Called store 6+ times						
Came to Design Night 1-2 times						
Came to Design Night 3-5 times						
Came to Design Night 6+ times						
Watched Design Night Webinar 1-2 times						
Watched Design Night Webinar 3-5 times						
Watched Design Night Webinar 6+ times						

Figure A-4. SPC customer activities-offers matrix

Resources Required

SPC knew that marketing was going to be a critical project for their sales in the next three months. So the owners agreed that one would spend a dedicated two to three hours every morning planning activities and doing analyses, while the other would spend two to three hours every afternoon and evening doing the activities (such as calling the contacts at the universities that the morning officer had obtained).

They understood that this meant they'd need to be getting up somewhat earlier and going to bed somewhat later for at least a few weeks, while they got their system and programs organized.

SPC also realized that they couldn't do all of their marketing using just their current staff, no matter how late into the night they worked. So they made the following choices.

- Hired a local high school student to maintain their web store
- Hired a local college art student to do their advertising layouts
- Hired local junior high school and college students to post flyers on a temporary basis
- Added one staff member to their counter staff, and altered others' hours so that each would work for two hours per day on various marketing projects—from setting up "design night" (ordering pizza, confirming the speakers) to entering the data collected at the register into a computer spreadsheet, to composing the store's electronic newsletter.

Cash Budget

The cash budget consists of the following elements:

- Raw materials for giveaway shirts: $700
- Stickers: $300
- Art nights: $500 each for food
- Newspaper and directory advertising: $1,400 (per quarter)
- Web hosting and site maintenance: $250 (per quarter)
- Street fair space, tent: $2,100
- Phone number: $100 (per quarter)
- Web coder and graphic artist: $2,400

Timeline

Given their critical dependencies, SPC's timeline looked like the following:

- **Week 1**: Analysis and plans outlined. New web layout sketched. Hire web coder and graphic artist from local school. Phone system changes and new number ordered. Checkout counter starts tracking purchasers. Call street fairs.
- **Week 2**: Analysis and plans done. Start calling existing artists and

speakers for "design night." Call college newspapers to obtain ad specifications. Layout initial sticker designs and send to printer. Call layout ad designs.

▶ **Week 3:** Phone system in place. Web redesign done, new content posted on Blog and artist area. Friends and family e-mail created and sent. Start running print ads and doing postering.

▶ **Week 4:** Send SPC monthly e-newsletter, and make print copies available at front desk, listing upcoming events.

▶ **Week 5:** Design Night 1 (pack with friends and family). Start contacting local bloggers based on design night survey results.

▶ **Week 6:** Street Fair 1. Design Night 2.

▶ **Week 7:** Send SPC monthly e-newsletter, and make print copies available at front desk, listing upcoming events.

▶ **Week 8:** Design Night 3.

▶ **Week 9:** Street Fair 2.

▶ **Week 10:** Design Night 4. Send SPC monthly e-newsletter, and make print copies available at front desk, listing upcoming events.

▶ **Week 11:** Send e-mail "last chance" reminder to promotion e-mail list.

Metrics and Goals

Based on their calculations, SPC sought to obtain the following:

▶ 8,330,000 "impressions" through ads

▶ 1,042 more visitors over the quarter

▶ 64 more sales per week at the average deal size of $30 (3 T-shirts)

Marketing Programs Plan: ServiceGroupInc

If your business is service-based—if you're either an independent professional, small business, or member of a larger company (or franchise) that sells things that you and your staff *do* for other people, such as dentistry, dry cleaning, food preparation/restauranteuring, lawn and garden care, house painting, accounting and tax preparation, or the like—then this marketing programs plan is for you. ServiceGroupInc is represented as a dentist's office, but the general form of their marketing plan and tactics could be adapted to any service business.

Context: ServiceGroupInc (SGI) is a (hypothetical) dental office in San Francisco, CA that provides family dental care. The owner of SGI would like to increase sales over the next three months.

Situation Analysis and Conclusions

SGI took three weeks to perform their initial marketing plan analysis. While this may seem like an extended period of time, SGI realized in the first few days that they didn't have much data on their competitors—so they had to spend more time on the phone finding people (their clients and friends, and friends of their clients) who were using other dental groups. SGI did *not* spend thousands of dollars and months of work on their plan—but they could easily have done so if they'd desired, by hiring a professional market research company to ask the same questions SGI was asking. If SGI had taken the professional approach, they would certainly have gotten more detailed data and taken less of the SGI staff time.

3 C/4 P Analysis

SGI started their analysis by building a 3 C/4 P matrix and studying their situation relative to those of the other dental providers in the area.

SGI had known that the local market for services contained three groups:

▶ National "chain" providers such as NationalDental and FreeClinic, whose dentists were local but whose office rentals, billing, supplies, pricing, and marketing were all coordinated by a central corporation;

▶ Local individual dentists, such as MomsDental and PopsDental, who had been in practice for many years, and provided primarily preventive care and basic services (cavity fillings, cleanings). Mom and Pop tended to have strengths in their cultural relationships (spoke local languages, etc.); and

▶ Small practices like SGI, which consisted of several less-well-established dentists. SGI and HospitalDental hoped to grow to become larger practices—if they didn't, they'd likely lose partners and look like Mom and Pop after another ten years.

Examining their pricing, SGI noticed that while the most common patient visit was for standard preventative care, most money was made out of cosmetic dentistry—teeth whitening, alignment, and tooth "patching" to create "perfect smiles." SGI suspected that they were well positioned to take advantage of the cosmetic market need, as their customer base was neither the price-sensitive group who visited the most convenient dental center (classic "chain" customers) nor the older, married couples who were well established with their dentist (and often felt less need for cosmetic dentistry).

[**Author's note:** If generalized, this segmentation could equally well apply to other service businesses such as dry cleaning and house painting—there's often a national "budget" franchise supplier, a few traditional suppliers, and a few newer businesses. As a newer business, your challenge is to find a unique space not already well served. This could be the income-differentiated detail-oriented customers, who are willing to pay extra to have *perfect* shirts or houses; the culturally differentiated customers, who want someone who speaks their language and practices business in a familiar style, or the age- or gender-differentiated customers, who'd prefer to do business with someone who understands their unique needs. Listen for the complaints about current businesses.]

SWOT Analysis

Strengths	**Weaknesses**
▪ Technologically savvy ▪ Able to specialize, not tied to chain ▪ Established practice with cosmetic skills	▪ Higher overhead costs than chains ▪ No 20-year established reputation ▪ Crowded market—all look the same
Opportunities	**Threats**
▪ Not doing any promotion currently ▪ High margins in the cosmetic business ▪ No one has hospital, fashion referrals	▪ Specialization in cosmetics costs more ▪ If no exclusivity in referrals, no win ▪ Price pressure from big chains

Figure A-5. SGI SWOT analysis

The subsequent SWOT analysis was taken from the initial 3 C/4 P analysis.

What the SWOT analysis suggested was that the way to increase sales was to appeal to the fashion-sensitive, higher-income group of customers. There were three ways to make that appeal—through direct marketing, affinity group marketing, and complementary-service marketing partners such as local cosmetic surgeons and hospital reconstructive centers.

Customer Purchase Process

Finally, the customer purchase process showed two areas of friction—the initial awareness of SGI, but also the transition from "evaluation" (people who made one "trial" visit to SGI for a consultation or cleaning) to repeat purchase. On further investigation, SGI determined that their desired high-end clientele didn't see significant differentiation between SGI's offerings and that of other dental practitioners. Changes in the actual product offering (service) would need to be made. As part of their preparations for their marketing programs, SGI changed their office layout. They put massage units and paraffin hand treatments in their dental chairs, added audio and DVD headsets, and put fountains and soft lighting in their waiting area. A separate sound-proofed waiting room with a monitor was created for families with children. The net result was an experience that SGI labeled "Spa Dentistry"—a service that approached dentistry as a self-pampering cosmetic service for high-value clientele. It was this new offering that SGI would market via their programs.

Marketing Program(s) Objective

Every marketing program should have a specific objective: Why are you doing these programs (versus other programs)? The objective should refer to situation analysis and customer purchase process—Is the aim to "increase awareness" or "move to purchase"?

Quantity versus Quality

SGI knew that they needed to raise sales—so quantity of customers was certainly a primary goal. Yet SGI had limited resources—they only had a limited number of dental practitioners and staff. So ideally every staff member would be seeing only high-value cosmetic customers. SGI decided to take a somewhat focused, "highest quantity *of a certain quality level* of customer" approach to their marketing. They knew that their cost per acquired customer might increase relative to their current spending—but they also knew that if they acquired the right high-quality cosmetic customers, the value of each customer would be three to five times their low-value customers, justifying the slightly higher costs of attracting them.

Choosing Goals

SGI was currently making about $1,200,000 per year in sales. They felt it would not be unreasonable to attempt a 30 percent increase in sales over the next three months—for an increase in yearly revenues of $400,000 (30 percent of $1,200,000).

Since three months was a quarter of a year, they'd need to see revenues of one-quarter of $400,000, or about $100,000 in additional sales.

SGI's average deal size was $200 (a standard cleaning), so they'd need to achieve an additional 1,000 deals, or about 80 more deals per week *if they didn't attract higher-value customers*. Yet their strategy was to pursue cosmetic customers, who were worth about $900 per deal. Since they hoped to make half of their new customers cosmetic, they expected an average deal size of $500 (400 + 200/2), meaning they'd need about 200 new deals, or about two a day.

Based on their ratio of "people who made appointments" to "people who actually showed up and paid for the service"—a 3-to-2 ratio—SGI assumed they'd need to get 200 times (3/2) additional people (300 people) to make appointments.

Based on the data obtained from their cosmetic surgery colleagues on likely response rate, SGI assumed that only 3 of every 100 people they could get mailing addresses for would show up at their shop—so they needed at least 10,000 contact addresses to solicit for appointments.

Finally, SGI knew from reading local cosmetic trade magazines and listening to the advertising guarantees of various dating web sites that they should expect no more than 0.1 percent (1 of every 1,000 people) exposed to their advertising to provide a contact address (via click through on a web banner, telephone call, or visit in response to the newspaper ad). So they needed to create about 10,000,000 "impressions" with their ads—or figure out a more effective awareness mechanism.

Tracking and Measuring

Since SGI had done very little awareness generation to date, they knew it would be critical to understand which activities worked and which didn't. They invested in three basic tracking mechanisms.

First, for less than $100, they purchased a new phone number with multi-extension capability. When people dialed the new, memorable number (1-800-my-smiles), they heard a greeting asking them to enter their extension or wait to leave a message on the general mailbox. All extensions actually rang through to the store, but SGI could examine the phone records later to understand who called extension 123 (the number listed on their postcards) and who called extension 567 (the number listed on their corporate brochures).

Second, SGI started using "promo codes" on every brochure or postcard they handed out. Each referring agency, corporate presentation, or other presentation was coded with a different number, and the cards promised benefits to the referring agencies when customers returned the cards.

Third, SGI asked their counter staff to ask every person who came to their clinic "how did you hear about us" and check off the appropriate boxes on a survey form at the front desk (person's name and address optional, but they were entered in a drawing for free care if they provided the information). This information was entered with the patient's record of treatment in SGI's computer system, so that they could understand where their high-value patients were coming from.

By implementing these three techniques, SGI felt that they'd have a much more detailed sense of which awareness techniques drove purchasers to their practice.

Marketing Programs Plan/Key Elements

SGI had chosen to appeal to the fashion-sensitive, higher-income group of customers through direct marketing, affinity-group marketing, and complementary-service marketing partners such as local cosmetic surgeons and hospital reconstructive centers.

Their plan included the following elements.

Friends and Family

Since SGI was attempting to build a professional, high-quality image, they couldn't risk overwhelming their clients with marketing materials or Tupperware-style multi-level marketing. Nonetheless, the basic friends and family referral concepts still applied, though offered in a different way.

- ▶ **Direct referral program:** SGI printed sophisticated, understated, heavy-card-stock business cards with a space on the back marked "referred by." Three of these cards, filled in with the patient's name, were handed to each patient as they left—along with a short personally signed note from the doctor explaining that SGI appreciated their business, valued referrals, and as a token of appreciation would be offering a gift certificate at a local spa or restaurant for every referral. This program was also announced in a single e-mail to their clients, phrased as a personal note from their leading doctor.

- ▶ **Transmissible item:** SGI was able to find a manufacturer who would create a thousand imprinted mirrored sticky-note pads for less than $500.

Each pad had a reflective mini-mirrored area on the top. The imprint on the pad was small, but said simply "Like your smile? We make smiles perfect. SGI Dental, 1-800-My-Smiles, specializing in cosmetic dentistry in a spa environment." While SGI acknowledged that they were risking their high-end image slightly by using sticky-notes, they felt that the items were sufficiently professionally created to mitigate that risk, were highly transmissible (one pad user would hand notes to quite a few people), and would reach the target audience if made available at cosmetician and fashion offices. (See below.)

▶ **Newsletter:** SGI agreed that they would create and send a monthly newsletter with appropriate cosmetic tips, reminders, and new service discussions.

Community

SGI's appeal to their community was similarly more subtle than SPC's in the analysis above—but more critical, as SGI depended on referrals from other practices.

▶ **Corporate program:** SGI created a presentation designed to explain various dental care options to employees of local large companies. While relatively unbiased in its presentation of the facts, the presentation did feature SGI's address, rates, and what was covered by local plans. SGI contacted the local Human Resources directors at the corporations, mentioned that SGI served patients who were employees, and offered to give free presentations in the corporate cafeteria.

▶ **Fashion program:** SGI contacted several local modeling agencies and cosmeticians, and offered a referral bonus to the businesses for every person they referred to SGI. SGI gave the agencies appropriate literature, lipstick cases to present to clients, and customized referral cards for their reception areas.

▶ **Medical program:** As with the fashion agencies, SGI contacted several local hospitals and cosmetic surgery physicians' offices, and offered to cross-refer for every person they referred to SGI, giving the agencies appropriate literature and customized referral cards for their reception areas. The primary difference in approach was in the nature of the literature. The fashion program literature emphasized the career-furthering aspects of SGI's dental work, and the discussion with the agencies was about revenue sharing. In contrast, the medical program literature emphasized the medical benefits and rejuvenating effects of SGI's work, and the discussion with the physicians' offices was about cross-referring patients.

▶ **Online seeding:** SGI hired a local college student who was familiar with the modeling industry to find all local online forums for fashion and modeling. The student found 10 blogs, 50 commercial company sites, and 4 discussion boards. SGI then gave the student a list of four points to make, about the advantages of cosmetic dentistry and success stories of people who'd visited SGI, and had the student start participating in the discussion boards, answering dental questions (answered by SGI's doctors) and periodically posting plaudits about SGI (with their phone number and e-mail address). SGI also approached the bloggers, explaining the SGI approach to "spa dentistry," and offering a trial of SGI's services in exchange for reviews on the site. SGI hoped to develop ongoing relationships with the bloggers, where SGI would be publicized in exchange for being available to answer cosmetic dentistry questions.

Awareness Programs

SGI had to strike a balance in tone between professionalism and visibility. Since their targeted client base was smaller and more local, SGI chose to spend more money on smaller, more focused awareness techniques, eschewing some of the more general approaches.

▶ **Advertising:** SGI chose not to engage in major billboards, television, or radio ads. Instead, SGI primarily created glossy fliers for their in-person corporate appearances, direct mailers, fashion partners, and medical partners. Additionally, they did place a print advertisement in the course catalog of a local modeling school.

▶ **Direct mail:** SGI avoided telemarketing, reasoning that its image was not consistent with SGI's desired image, and thus that they'd likely not recoup the cost with a commensurate number of patients. But SGI did produce subtle, understated direct-mail items, "introducing their dental practice," and inviting recipients to experience spa dentistry at their convenience. These letters were mailed to several lists—those obtained from SGI's fashion and medical partners, and those obtained from a local list broker, listing "high-value professionals" in the local Zip codes. The lists were expensive to acquire, but SGI's funnel math calculations led them to believe that the ROI would be quite positive.

▶ **News and PR:** SGI contacted local newspapers, fashion magazines, and the newsletter departments of the local hospitals and medical organizations with a press release and prewritten articles on the new trend in "spa dentistry." Phrased as a human interest piece for the newspapers, and a medical approach breakthrough (a more relaxing environment reducing perceived pain and stress) for the medical groups, SGI hoped to gain placement. SGI also contacted the calendar groups of each vehicle, listing their "open houses"/lectures on spa dentistry at various corporations.

▶ **Directories and online search presence:** SGI spent large amounts of money on availability. They purchased large, though professional and understated advertisements in directories issued by modeling agencies to their clients, as well as physicians' listings by local HMO and PPO groups, and "yellow pages" consumer guide listings in all available local directories, including local college directories. Also, they leased the terms "spa dentistry" and "cosmetic dentistry" for the "local search" option on several Internet search engines.

▶ **Shows:** SGI arranged for a booth at every local fashion industry show and "health fair," spending on large poster signs at the fashion shows.

Partnering

SGI knew that their partners, the fashion agencies and medical groups, would be critical to their success—and so SGI designed marketing *to* those groups, as well as ways to maintain a tighter relationship.

▶ **Bundling:** SGI arranged a cross-billing arrangement with a local cosmetic surgery practice, so that patients who visited both facilities would only get one bill, submitted once to their insurance company. By being co-listed, SGI hoped that they'd remove some barriers to patients' use of their services.

Dependencies

When SGI reviewed their tasks, they realized that there were a few critical projects that needed to be completed before they could launch the remainder of their activities—which could then be launched in any order.

▶ Their infrastructure—phone number, space for marketing referral source in their reception computer records, new "spa dentistry" type of office—had to be in place first, as all printed materials would point people to those points of contact.

▶ Their flyers and materials for corporate presentations had to be created.

The remainder of their marketing—arranging the relationships with the fashion and medical groups, setting up corporate lectures, and so forth—could all follow.

Resources

SGI knew that marketing was going to be a critical project for their sales in the next three months. Since the physicians running the practice didn't have time available during the week to dedicate to the marketing, they agreed that they'd work together each Saturday for a few weeks to get the initial plans in place, then hire a part-time "marketing contractor" for the quarter to execute their plans (including visiting the medical and fashion groups) and assist in their strategy, by advertising at a local business school.

Cash Budget

▶ Printed referral program cards: $300

▶ Mirrored pads: $460

▶ Sponsored lunches: $500 each for food

▶ Online seeding hire: $300/month

▶ Printed glossy brochures: $1,200

▶ Directory and search advertising: $2,700 (per quarter)

▶ Direct-mail piece: $730

▶ Web hosting and site maintenance: $250 (per quarter)

▶ Phone number: $100 (per quarter)

▶ Fashion show presence (including table): $2,300

▶ Marketing contractor: $3,500 / month

Timeline

Given their critical dependencies, SGI's timeline looked like this:

▶ **Week 1**: Analysis and plans outlined. New phone number ordered. Front desk system starts tracking referral sources. Draft PowerPoint presentation and text for flyers created. Local design/print company hired to clean up the presentation and flyer and print professional versions, as well as several runs of reference cards (with different referral codes). Marketing contractor hired.

▶ **Week 2:** Analysis and plans done. Engage sticky-note creators. Start calling corporations for appointments, also health fairs, medical groups, and fashion businesses. Call modeling school for ad specs and layout ad designs. Contact direct-mail brokerage.

▶ **Week 3:** Direct-mail content created. Begin corporate and other presentations. Have contractor hire "online community" seeder. Contract for ads in directories. Start show setup.

▶ **Week 4:** Create article. Contact newspapers, PR for the medical groups. Send first electronic newsletter, making print copies available in reception areas of SGI and fashion/medical group partners.

▶ **Week 5:** Direct mail goes out.

▶ **Week 6:** Check into status of fashion, medical referrals—number of sticky-pads and referral cards handed out, number of responses seen.

▶ **Week 7:** First shows.

▶ **Week 8:** Send monthly newsletter.

▶ **Weeks 9-13:** Repeat presentations, direct mail, newsletter, and shows.

Metrics and Goals

Based on their calculations, SGI sought to obtain:

▶ 10,000,000 "impressions" through referrals and directory placement

▶ 300 new appointments booked

▶ 200 actual new client visits, at an average of 50 percent cosmetic, for an average $500 bill

Appendix B

Common Tools

"The best strategy in life is diligence."

—Chinese Proverb

MANY BRILLIANT ENTREPRENEURIAL MARKETING PLANS HAVE failed due to poor execution. It's much simpler to *say* "let's create a seminar series" than to actually *create* a successful series. Especially if operating on a shoestring budget, where all activities must be executed by you or your staff—or where you must strike hard bargains with contractors—it's critical that you understand the details of program execution.

This appendix presents details of some of the most common tactical tools needed to successfully implement marketing plans. You'll get a checklist of activities, a sense of timing and flow, and warning notes on areas that can cause problems. If you read any section of the appendix, it should provide you with a great starting point on making your program work flawlessly.

Tactical challenges covered include:

▶ Printed materials (Collateral)
▶ Sales tools
▶ Measurement tools
▶ Automated customer interaction systems

- ▸ Infrastructure partners
- ▸ Sales and marketing partners

Printed Materials

An entrepreneurial marketer stranded on a desert island could come up with great supporting materials given just a copy of Microsoft PowerPoint, Adobe Acrobat, and his imagination. Most customers want to know just three things about your business (product or service)—what does it do, how will it help me, and how much will it cost. All other questions—such as in which environment it needs to run effectively, what supplies and services it needs, how it will interact with other products, and how it compares with other similar products—are variations on the primary three themes.

Correspondingly, lead-generation managers should always have the following documents available to their customers and sales teams:

- ▸ **Product presentations:** Presented as a series of annotated slides describing the company, product, application of the product, and benefits to the end consumer. Do you need these even if you're a business as simple as a fast-food restaurant or dry cleaning business? Absolutely—it's called a menu or brochure, with photos of what you can deliver on it. Visual presentation of what customers get is always a good thing.

- ▸ **Roadmap presentations:** A presentation similar to the product presentation, presenting the overview and direction of the product and company. It should be futures-oriented. Again, if you're a fast-food restaurant, this may be less necessary—but a "coming soon" sign is the equivalent.

- ▸ **Datasheets:** This is typically one or two full-page synopses of the product aspects presented in the product presentation, as well as additional detailed relevant product/environmental specifications, such as dimensions, operating environment, and prerequisites. The simple example of this is the nutritional information at the restaurant (which may be exposed in detail, or simply as a star next to the spicy or low-cal items on the menu, or not exposed at all unless customers request it).

- ▸ **Comparative or competitive studies:** These are usually multi-page written documents containing comparative tables, performance graphs, survey evidence, and other evidence to prove the superiority of your product relative to others. They can also be presented as a slide presen-

An entrepreneurial marketer stranded on a desert island could come up with great supporting materials given just a copy of Microsoft PowerPoint, Adobe Acrobat, and his imagination.

tation. The simple example of this would be visual demonstrations of how much bigger your fast-food meals are, or how much lower your prices are, or how much cleaner your dry-cleaned shirts are in a side-by-side comparison.

▶ **ROI analysis:** The return on investment analysis is a study of financial costs and benefits of purchasing your product, presented in a form similar to that of the comparative studies.

▶ **Whitepaper(s):** This is a multi-page, more detailed writeup and study of aspects of your product, presented from a focused viewpoint of one of your customer's areas of concern. For example, an automobile might have a whitepaper discussing its engine specifications and performance, a whitepaper discussing its safety features, a whitepaper discussing its economy and cost efficiency, and a whitepaper discussing its environmental impact.

▶ **Calculators:** Product performance and costs depend on usage. Customers prefer tailored estimates. The car example might give you a calculator showing your expected gasoline costs relative to the competitors if you entered your daily commute profile (miles, highway versus street, during rush hours or not). A diet food might offer likely pounds lost based on eating inputs.

In short, be prepared to answer questions.

Sales Tools

Since sales' primary focus is selling, not learning more about your products, materials for sales need to be designed for quick study and repetition, or to guide sales to guide customers.

Just as customers need answers, so too do salespeople need materials guiding them in giving correct answers. Since sales' primary focus is selling, not learning more about your products, materials for sales need to be designed for quick study and repetition, or to guide sales to guide customers. Sales teams act as an index for customers to provide the correct materials. Don't think you have a sales team? If you have one staff member other than yourself, or even customers who talk about your product to others, you have a sales team.

Correspondingly, arm your sales team with:

▶ **Sales cycle model:** What should they expect to be happening with prospects given the characteristics of your product? Should customers buy in hours or months? How will a salesperson know if their sale is lagging, and therefore need to be more involved?

- ▶ **Quick reference guides:** If a customer calls with interest about a product, the salesperson should be able to flip to a page in the book and read back a sales pitch for the product.

- ▶ **Frequently asked questions:** If a customer calls, the salesperson should easily be able to answer their questions and direct them to the appropriate materials.

- ▶ **Posters:** These can be left at a reseller, to provide unconscious learning for sales and customer self-service in conference rooms.

- ▶ **Audio CD:** When driving, salespeople can listen to a presentation narrated by marketing, and then be able to repeat it back. The CD should also work in a computer and contain the presentation text and graphics.

Demonstrations and Trial

A picture is worth a thousand words—and a hands-on trial is worth a thousand pictures. At a minimum, your lead-generation efforts should make visual demonstrations of your product available; ideally, hands-on trials would also occur.

Visual demonstrations can occur in many ways. Some methods include narrated video of your product in use (made available on videocassette or DVD mailed to customers, via Internet streaming video, digital file download, or digital file on CD), animated schematics, or even narrated (or static) photo slide shows or albums. From body waxing to real estate, delivery of physical video, photo albums, or electronic versions thereof have become common practice.

Trials can similarly occur in the real or virtual world, in destructive or nondestructive ways. A few examples include test-driving automobiles versus trying various levels of driving simulator; downloading time-limited "evaluation" copies of software, trying "sample size" detergent, or sampling tastes of foods at local stores. In all cases, the goal is to show the product to best advantage to prospective users—the use itself prequalifying, educating, influencing, and creating commitment on the part of the prospective customer.

Since both visual demonstrations and trials can be quite expensive (production and mailing of DVDs; onsite visits and physical degradation of physical products), it is wise to balance the compelling nature of the trial against the need to prequalify users prior to trial. Failing to prequalify a person downloading a free software trial is low risk—they'll qualify themselves through successful use of the product (or not). Failing to prequalify a test

*A*t a minimum, your lead-generation efforts should make visual demonstrations of your product available; ideally, hands-on trials would also occur.

driver of a new Lamborghini can have disastrous consequences, if the tester who wrecks the car turns out to have been an uninsured high-school student.

Automated Customer Interaction Systems

If a prospective customer is located in a different time zone—or perhaps just wakes up at two in the morning and has a sudden urge to buy or learn more about your products—you'd ideally have a cost-efficient way to serve that prospect and capture that potential lead. Automated systems range from recorded phone messages (voicemail menus), to fax-response systems, to Internet web pages and forms, to voice response phone systems. In all cases, the goal is to allow the customer to efficiently find and retrieve the information they want at any time.

Automated systems should be deployed to cover at least the following areas of infrastructure that will be needed for shoestring lead generation.

▶ **Initial response (landing pages):** When you contact your target audience to make them aware of your company and offering, you provide them with a "call to action". Ideally, they heed this call to action, and respond to your company. While the response may take the form of a physical response postcard or phone call requiring human interaction (see the section on partnering, below), ideally their response could be handled in a scaleable, low-cost way. Consider phone systems that allow respondents to key in or speak a unique response code to confirm their interest or obtain materials, or Internet-based web forms or click-through URLs.

▶ **Educational materials:** When your target audience responds, they'll be seeking additional educational information as well. A phone-based (recorded), fax, or e-mail system, or Internet-based system for providing information is scaleable. The Internet system has the added benefit of being able to display video or animation, and provide information brochures in downloadable form at a fraction of the cost of mailing printed information.

▶ **Contact capture (registration):** At trade shows, contact information may be captured via electronic card-readers—and at point-of-sale, clerks can enter purchaser information. But outside of those two forums, reply cards (mailed or faxed in) or Internet forms are the leading mechanisms, and only the latter is free of human intervention. Especially if launching a seminar or seminar series, online registration lowers costs.

If a prospective customer wakes up at two in the morning and has a sudden urge to buy or learn more about your products—you'd ideally have a cost-efficient way to serve that prospect and capture that potential lead.

- ▶ **Qualification (survey):** The extended form of contact capture, surveying, or asking additional questions when obtaining contact information, is essential to the lead-generation and qualification process. Whether the surveying is implicit, based on monitoring purchase patterns, or explicit, asking questions, standardization via electronic entry and storage is essential.

- ▶ **Trial:** If possible, trial should be at least requested via the mechanisms above.

- ▶ **Purchase:** Buying via credit card "online" depends on the product. Of course, communication with resellers should be via a (password-protected) partner web site!

- ▶ **Post-purchase (rebate):** Outsource and/or automate rebates, if possible, linking them directly from a point of sales (POS) device ("cash register") to an online web page, so that people don't need to go through a cumbersome "fill in this form and mail it in" process. See for example Staples, Inc., which allows for instantaneous tracking of your rebates— go buy something and see!

In all cases, the automated system functions could also be performed by live representatives of your company—and in many cases, given sufficient customer interest and lead volume, it will make financial sense to staff accordingly to preserve customer goodwill—but to maximize leverage, for coverage above a certain volume of potential lead flow, automation is essential.

Vendor/Supplier Partners

The above systems may be implemented by your company. But depending on the scale of your lead flow, you may choose to outsource certain functions. Above functions that are non-core to most companies (e.g., if you're not in the seminar business, then hosting an online seminar registration system is likely non-core) include:

- ▶ *Online survey systems*
- ▶ *Online event registration systems*
- ▶ *Fax-back systems*
- ▶ *Voice-response or menu-driven voice systems*
- ▶ *High-volume outbound e-mail systems*

▶ *Online rebate systems*

▶ *Online storage/high-bandwidth hosting for downloadable materials*

In addition, you may wish to engage partners for such non-online, non-core lead-generation functions as:

▶ **Marketing material creation:** Unless you have a particularly talented staff member who is willing to moonlight as a graphic artist, or you have an inordinately high flow of programs, it may make sense to outsource the formatting, graphics, design, and actual printing of datasheets and informational materials. You and your team create the text and information; they create the physical form.

▶ **Physical marketing material fulfillment:** Especially for smaller lead-generation programs, it may be more efficient to have a third party send your seminar invitations, or respond to prospective customer requests for whitepapers or other materials. Your job is again about customer information; they handle logistics of materials delivery. Everyone is happier.

▶ **Rebate processing and fulfillment:** Given the increasing complexity of rebates from a financial and legal compliance perspective, coupled with the labor-intensive nature of rebate processing, it likely makes sense to outsource rebate processing to a dedicated group.

To accomplish the necessary communication with your supplier partners, online communication will also be necessary.

Sales and Marketing Partners

John Donne wrote "No man is an island"—and the same is true of lead-generating companies. Regardless of the size of your company or the industry in which you operate, your company will be affiliated with others who participate in your lead-generation process. At a minimum, excluding suppliers as discussed above, your company will likely have at least three types of relationships—some of which will apply simultaneously to a partner: cooperative alliances (co-marketing, co-sales), resellers of your product, and suppliers of leads.

Resellers of your product are extensions of your sales team. These partners can range from logistics and distribution partners, as Wal-Mart is for many consumer goods companies, to value-added resellers, as systems consulting firms are to many computer software and hardware companies. In a reseller situation, your lead-generation efforts are the primary influence on

Regardless of the size of your company or the industry in which you operate, your company will be affiliated with others who participate in your lead-generation process.

the customer—your materials educate the customer, your campaigns make the customer aware of your offering, and in many cases, your contact and qualification systems process leads, which are turned over to the reseller for actual sale and closure. Even if the reseller handles aspects of lead generation, your responsibility is to support them, like your sales force. You need the same or better levels of communication with them as with your sales team. Assume you need routine conference calls and a private Internet site with downloadable sales guides for them. Give them as much advance notice as possible of impending company changes—from product launches to company changes. They need to be as aware as your sales team of issues that will affect your customers. That said, like your sales force, you should be aware of the possibility for "leaks" of announcements—and you should also demand accountability for leads. A partner who isn't producing sales based on your leads isn't a partner, and shouldn't be recognized as one.

If you are reselling another company's product, recognize the relationship just described and invert it. You should not be spending your own lead-generation efforts on their product. You should be doing lead generation for your product or service, and including theirs to the extent that it's a part of your offering.

If you are in a cooperative or peer alliance, only then should your lead-generation efforts be equally balanced. In a symbiotic or co-branded relationship, such as that between many computer hardware manufacturers, Microsoft, and Intel, each participant's efforts benefit all sides. Demand accountability, but provide it as well.

Index